Ordnance Survey

KU-064-713

LAKE DISTRICT

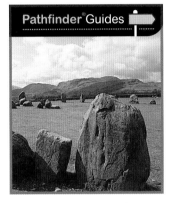

Pathfinder® Guides

Outstanding
Circular Walks

Compiled by
Terry Marsh

Text:	Terry Marsh
Photography:	Terry Marsh
Editorial:	Ark Creative (UK) Ltd
Design:	Ark Creative (UK) Ltd

© Crown copyright / Ordnance Survey Limited, 2018
Published by Crimson Publishing Ltd under licence from Ordnance Survey Limited.
Pathfinder, Ordnance Survey, OS and the OS logos are registered trademarks of
Ordnance Survey Limited and are used under licence from Ordnance Survey Limited.
Text © Crimson Publishing Limited, 2018

This product includes mapping data licensed from Ordnance Survey
© Crown copyright and database rights (2018) OS 150002047

ISBN 978-0-319-09016-9

This edition first published in Great Britain 2009 by Crimson Publishing. Reprinted
with amendments in 2012, 2014, 2015, 2016, 2017 (twice) and 2018.

Crimson Publishing, 19-21C Charles Street, Bath, BA1 1HX

www.pathfinderwalks.co.uk

Printed in India by Replika Press Pvt. Ltd. 8/18

A catalogue record for this book is available from the British Library.

Front cover: The Langdale Pikes and the River Brathay
Previous page: Castlerigg Stone Circle

Contents

Safety on the Hills;
Walkers and the Law;
Countryside Access Charter;
Useful Organisations;
Ordnance Survey Maps

Approximate walk times

 Up to 2½ hours   *3–3½ hours*   *4 hours and over*

The walk times are provided as a guide only and are calculated using an average walking speed of 2½mph (4km/h), adding one minute for each 10m (33ft) of ascent, and then rounding the result to the nearest half hour.

Keymap

WORKINGTON

Flimby
Seaton
Siddick
Great Clifton
Stainburn
High Harrington
Harrington
Grayson Green
Distington
Common End
Gilgarran
Lowca
Howgate
Parton
Moresby
Low Moresby
Moresby Parks
Arlecdon
Rowrah
Frizington
WHITEHAVEN
Sandwith
Rottington
St Bees
EGREMONT
Coulderton
Middletown
Nethertown
Beckermet
Braystones
CLEATOR MOOR
Moor Row
Bigrigg
Cleator
Thornhill
Haile
Calder Bridge
Gosforth
Sellafield Sta
Seascale
Holmrook
Drigg
Gubbergill
Ravenglass
Muncaster Castle
ROMAN BATH HOUSE
Broad Oak
Waberthwaite
Lane End
Corney
Prior Park
Stubb Place
Hycemoor
Bootle Station
Bootle
Annaside
Whitbeck
Silecroft
Kirksanton
Whicham
MILLOM

Broughton Moor
Great Broughton
Dovenby
Camerton
Bridekirk
Papcastle
COCKERMOUTH
Dubwath
Brigham
Greysouthen
Bridgefoot
Eaglesfield
Deanscales
Dean
Branthwaite
Ullock
Pardshaw
Mockerkin
Embleton
Wadcrag
Lorton
Lord's Seat
Whinlatter Pass
Thornth
Braithwaite
Grisedale Pike
Lamplugh
Loweswater
Loweswater Fell
Loweswater
Grasmoor
Causey Pike
Kirkland
Croasdale
Ennerdale Bridge
Murton Fell
Great Borne
Buttermere
Derwent Fells
Newlands Hause
Grike
ENNERDALE WATER
Ennerdale Fell
Red Pike
High Sti
Buttermere Fell
Honister Pass
Seatoller
Lank Rigg
Pillar
Scoat Fell
Black Sail Pass
Seathwaite
Caw Fell
Haycock
Kirk Fell
Great Gable
Seatallan
COPELAND FOREST
Wasdale Head
Lingmell
Great End
SCAFELL PIKE
Nether Wasdale
WAST WATER
The Screes
ROMAN FORT
Boot
Hardknott Pass
Santon Bridge
Beckfoot
Eskdale
Harter Fell
Eskdale Green
Stanley Force
Devoke Water
Seath
Hall Dunnerdale
Woodend
Ulpha Fell
Ulpha
Stickle Pike
Hoses
Whitfell
Dunnerdale
Corney
Broughton Mills
Stoneside Hill
Bootle Fell
Duddon Bridge
Lower Hawthwaite
Broughton in Furnes
Black Combe
Hallthwaites
The Green
Green Road Station
Foxfield
The Hill
Kirkby-in-Furness
Soutergate

Tallentire
Sunderland
Blindcrake
Isel Hall
Bewaldeth
Binsey

Roman Road
A594
A595
A596
A597
A66
A59
A5086
A5344
A5093
A593
B5292
B5289
B5294
B5345

Kokoarrah
Tarn Bay
Selker Bay
Moss Bay

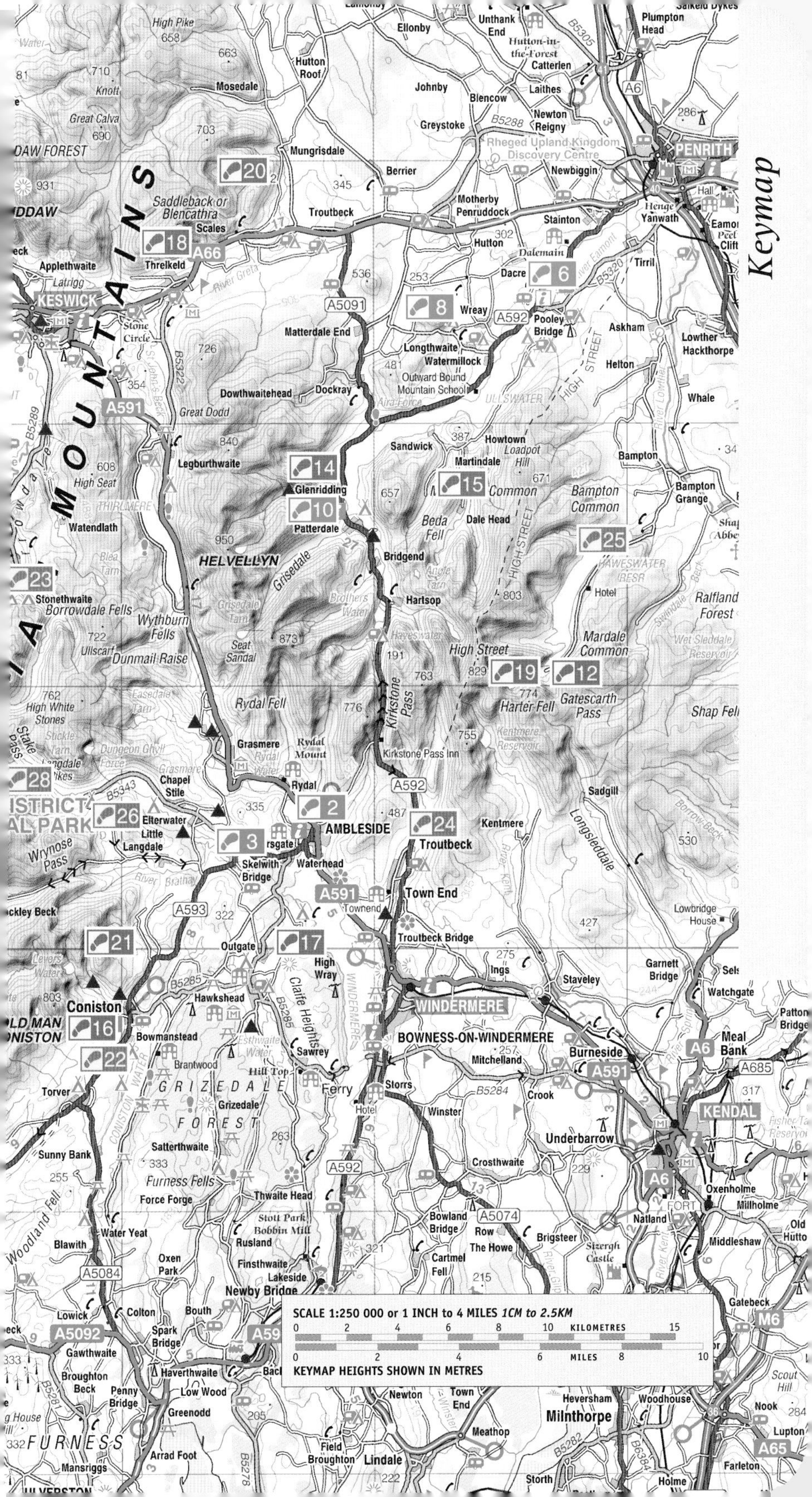

Keymap

PENRITH

KESWICK

MOUNTAINS

HELVELLYN

AMBLESIDE

WINDERMERE

BOWNESS-ON-WINDERMERE

KENDAL

Coniston

Saddleback or Blencathra

Grasmere

Troutbeck

Patterdale

Glenridding

Pooley Bridge

Kirkstone Pass

High Street

Mardale Common

Bampton Common

Ralfland Forest

Shap Fells

FURNESS

Newby Bridge

Milnthorpe

Walk	Page	Start	Nat. Grid Reference	Distance	Time	Height Gain
Bannerdale Crags and Souther Fell	60	Mungrisdale	NY 364302	6¾ miles (10.8km)	3½ hrs	2,015ft (614m)
Beda Fell	47	Martindale	NY 433190	5½ miles (9km)	3 hrs	1,510ft (460m)
Black Combe	86	Whicham	SD 135826	8½ miles (13.5km)	4½ hrs	2,185ft (666m)
Blencathra: Hall's Fell Ridge and Doddick Fell	55	Threlkeld	NY 324255	3¾ miles (6km)	3 hrs	2,395ft (730m)
Bowfell	89	Great Langdale	NY 286061	7½ miles (12km)	4½ hrs	2,855ft (870m)
Branstree and Selside Pike	39	Mardale Head	NY 469107	5½ miles (9.2km)	3 hrs	1,740ft (530m)
Buttermere	20	Buttermere	NY 173169	4½ miles (7km)	2 hrs	395ft (120m)
Cat Bells	18	Hawse End	NY 247212	3½ miles (5.6km)	2 hrs	1,150ft (350m)
Coniston Old Man	50	Coniston	SD 304975	5 miles (8km)	3 hrs	2,430ft (740m)
Dalemain and Dacre	22	Dalemain	NY 477270	4½ miles (7.25km)	2 hrs	445ft (135m)
Devoke Water	12	Birker Fell	SD 171977	3 miles (5km)	1½ hrs	490ft (150m)
Glenridding and Lanty's Tarn	33	Glenridding	NY 386169	5¼ miles (8.3km)	2½ hrs	1,015ft (310m)
Haweswater shore path	78	Burnbanks	NY 508161	10 miles (16.3km)	4½ hrs	1,273ft (388m)
Hay Stacks	42	Gatesgarth	NY 195150	4½ miles (7km)	3 hrs	1,870ft (570m)
The Langdale valleys	82	Great Langdale	NY 294064	8½ miles (13.5km)	4½ hrs	1,690ft (515m)
Little Mell Fell	28	Thackthwaite	NY 417252	4¼ miles (6.75km)	2½ hrs	1,065ft (325m)
Loughrigg Tarn and the Brathay	16	Silverthwaite	NY 341037	3 miles (4.6km)	1½ hrs	525ft (160m)
Loweswater	30	Loweswater	NY 135210	5½ miles (8.6km)	2½ hrs	885ft (270m)
Ravenglass and Muncaster	25	Ravenglass	SD 085964	4½ miles (7km)	2 hrs	670ft (210m)
Rosthwaite and Stonethwaite	70	Rosthwaite	NY 258148	9 miles (14.5km)	4 hrs	850ft (260m)
Rough Crag and High Street	58	Mardale Head	NY 469107	5½ miles (9km)	3½ hrs	2,100ft (640m)
Seathwaite Tarn	36	Seathwaite	SD 229962	4¾ miles (7.6km)	2½ hrs	1,065ft (325m)
Sheffield Pike and Glenridding Dodd	44	Glencoynedale	NY 386189	5 miles (8km)	3 hrs	1,935ft (590m)
Sweden Bridges	14	Ambleside	NY 377045	3 miles (5km)	1½ hrs	755ft (230m)
Torver Commons and Walna Scar	67	Coniston	SD 304975	8¼ miles (13.2km)	4 hrs	1,425ft (435m)
Troutbeck Valley	74	Troutbeck	NY 412 027	7¾ miles (12.5km)	4 hrs	1,330ft (405m)
Wetherlam	64	High Tilberthwaite	NY 306010	5½ miles (8.8km)	3½ hrs	2,295ft (700m)
Wray Castle and Blelham Tarn	52	High Wray	SD 385995	6 miles (9.7km)	3 hrs	785ft (240m)

A fine and energetic ascent, followed by a lovely valley descent before an easy pull onto a long grassy ridge reputably haunted by ghostly armies.

A splendid ridge walk high above Boredale and Bannerdale, culminating in a retreat through the latter; a peaceful and remote outing.

A wide and glorious exploration of the great swelling mound north of Millom that is Black Combe. The walk can be shortened by returning directly from the summit.

An energetic but superbly exhilarating rocky road to a stunning viewpoint, followed by an equally agreeable descent. Outstanding views throughout.

An ascent to the highest summit in Great Langdale, the popular and rewarding Bowfell. A rocky romp to an ancient thoroughfare, concluded by an easy and satisfying walk down one of Lakeland's great valleys.

Climbing steadily from the remote head of Mardale, the walk finds the easiest way onto Branstree to begin an easy and delightful amble across moorland tops.

An easy and very popular walk around one of Lakeland's finest tarns. With very little ascent, and a generally excellent footpath underfoot, this circuit is agreeable at any time of year.

A short, but stiff climb to an iconic summit overlooking Derwent Water and the valleys of Borrowdale and Newlands. An excellent half day's walk, with extensive views.

An up-and-down ascent of one of Lakeland's most popular fells, first ascended by a tourist in 1792. Quarry spoil mars much of the ascent, but the summit rewards with spectacular views.

There is so much history, antiquity and intrigue soaked into this walk there almost isn't enough time to do the walk.

Splendidly wild and untamed country amid lazy mountains and idling becks; extend or reduce the walk as you wish, but nothing will better a remote day around Devoke Water.

Launching itself from the tourist hotspot of Glenridding, the walk visits the site of the largest lead mine in the Lake District, before skipping southwards into Grisedale, by way of secluded Lanty's Tarn.

Although an entirely low-level walk, this circuit of Haweswater can be tiring. It uses a section of the popular Coast-to-Coast walk, and makes a splendid round for a long summer's day.

A fine walk to a shapely fell made popular by the late Alfred Wainwright, a place of tarns and crags, and continuing into a region of industrial heritage.

A superb walk around Great and Little Langdale, visiting remote tarns, prehistoric sites and one of the finest ancient packhorse bridges of Lakeland.

A surprisingly delightful romp along country lanes and across an isolated fell with an interesting geological history.

Loughrigg Tarn is easy on the eye and makes a most agreeable destination. Here the visit is extended to spend some time in company of the main river hereabouts, the Brathay.

A pleasing walk that makes use of a terraced path across the slopes of Burnbank Fell, and giving lovely views of Loweswater and out across the estuary of Solway Firth to the hills of southern Scotland.

Follow in the footsteps of Romans, and visit the ancestral home of an ancient family before striking across country to visit a remote corn mill.

A long but generally low-level walk of considerable glacial and geological interest, visiting the location of a number of post-glacial lakes.

A fine bumpy ridge rises steadily to the base of High Street from where a long pull leads onto the summit plateau. Easy strolling follows as the route descends to Mardale Ill Bell.

One of the finest lakeside settings anywhere, high above the Duddon valley and surrounded by outlying fells of the Coniston range. A return through streamside woodland brings you back to Dunnerdale.

A splendid walk through a secluded dale to an oft-neglected summit and neighbouring satellite, both of which provide outstanding views. The walk concludes through Mossdale, and a walk beside Ullswater.

Two ancient packhorse bridges are visited in this walk into a remote and tranquil valley that was once a thoroughfare across the fells into Patterdale.

A fine contrasting walk that begins along the shoreline of Coniston Water before climbing onto Torver Commons and the ancient packhorse route of Walna Scar.

Inviting exploration but invariably passed through, Troutbeck is a beautiful and easily explored dale, a conservation area endowed with vernacular architecture and associations with Beatrix Potter.

Wetherlam is a relatively neglected summit even though it has a grandstand view of the Old Man of Coniston and Swirl How, and its ascent begins in one of the least well-known dales in Lakeland.

A chance to explore the quiet side of Windermere, visit a fairy-tale castle, and the childhood summer residence of Beatrix Potter. Woodlands, tarns and lakeshore combine in a walk of tranquility.

Introduction to the Lake District

The Lake District attracts visitors from all around the world; more than 12 million visitors each year arrive in what was once called 'the odd corner of England'. They come for the outstanding quality of the landscape, and by doing so serve to endorse William Wordsworth's vision of a 'sort of national property, in which every man has a right and interest who has an eye to perceive and a heart to enjoy'.

Man has been in the region since prehistoric times, when the hunter-gatherers, who came in search of food, gradually settled and became the first farmers, and axe manufacturers. Later, the region attracted the Romans, who built forts and roads at strategic points. Then came Scandinavian invaders, mainly to the west coast, arriving from the Isle of Man in particular. And yet in spite of their extended stay over many centuries, there is comparatively little archaeological evidence of their presence. What does remain are the place-names, and many of the names of valleys, towns and villages have Scandinavian roots.

But the prominence of the region as a tourist destination was many years hence, its development hampered by the lack of roads. Some improvement came in the aftermath of the Jacobite Rebellion in 1745, which highlighted the need to establish good communication links between England and Scotland. By 1768, the main route through what was then Westmorland and Cumberland – now the A591 – was in place. It was the first of many new roads, turnpikes that were to follow.

The notion of the Lake District as one having a regional identity was first aroused by the poet Thomas Gray, who travelled through the Lakes in 1769, and saw the landscapes we see today as a work of art, describing them vividly in a series of letters to a friend. The letters were published after Gray's death and inspired Thomas West, a topographer and Jesuit-mission priest, to produce his *Guide to the Lakes* in 1778, a publication so avidly received that it ran to many editions. This was the first real tourist guidebook, albeit a weighty one – the first edition ran to more than 200 pages. In it West described 'stations' – increased in number in later editions – from which the best views could be obtained.

By the time revolution and war had rendered European travel unsafe, the middle and upper classes were looking northward for their recreation. Then it was, from the 1790s onward, that the Lake District began to see increasing numbers of visitors. Now guidebooks flowed ceaselessly from the presses, an incidence that has scarcely abated since.

The lakes are but one ingredient in the landscape of the Lake District – pedantically there is only one 'lake', Bassenthwaite Lake; all the others are

Cat Bells and Derwent Water from Watendlath

meres, tarns, waters, etc. The fells, which include the highest summit in England, along with the valleys, the towns and villages – almost 400 of them – all add weight to the vision of John Dower whose 1945 report augured the development of national parks as areas of 'beautiful and relatively wild country which should be preserved for the benefit of the nation'.

Dower's assessment was correct: this is a place of great diversity, a place of contrasts and harmonies, conflicts and tranquility, shade and light, a synergy of harmonious relationships, a whole that is far greater than the sum of its parts. It is a place of extremes, too: the longest and the deepest lakes in England, its highest mountains, the steepest roads (Hardknott Pass is 33%, or 1 in 3); St Olaf's Church in Wasdale is said to be the smallest church in England. And at Santon Bridge, each year sees the crowning of the World's Biggest Liar.

Few of the early Victorian visitors came to walk the fells; mostly they were content with visiting spas, like Shap Wells and Gilsland, both on the edge of Lakeland, or of taking tours offered by the new hotels that were developing, such as the Low Wood, and the Windermere Hotel. Recreational walking was in its infancy, and guidebooks specifically for walkers still to come.

Many of the early guidebooks gave details of walks that might be pursued, and local guides were quick to spot the profit in taking visitors on the backs of ponies up onto mountains like Helvellyn and Skiddaw. But the status of the Lakeland fells as walking destinations had begun many years earlier, probably beyond recall, although it is known that the Bishop of Carlisle ascended Skiddaw in the 17th-century purely for pleasure.

The modern cult for walking is popularly linked to the Romantic movement, spear-headed by Wordsworth. But it is more profound than this,

Looking across from Souther Fell to Bannerdale Crags

and there were enthusiasts, like Bishop Carlisle, who, in spite of lurid descriptions bestowed on mountainous country, were happy to temper their feelings of repugnance with a certain grudging admiration.

Contemporary with Wordsworth's youth, interest in the Lake District grew each year. For most visitors, mountains were no more than a backdrop, a lake accessory or adornment. But for a hardy few, the fells were beginning to attract. Cumberland historian, William Hutchinson, ascended Skiddaw in 1772 and 1773, doing so with a guide, who on the first occasion was reduced to a state of panic by a thunderstorm. Captain Joseph Budworth rambled through the Lakes in 1792 and 1795, covering more than 240 miles. Unaffected by the prevailing Romantic mood, he walked freely among the fells and trundled boulders down Helvellyn.

When the railway line to Windermere opened in April 1847, it heralded a new era of tourism, and a discernible change in the content of guidebooks. Harriet Martineau's excellent guidebook (c1864) contains a tourist map and a table of heights of the principal mountains. Murray's *Handbook to the English Lakes* (1889) is keen to emphasise how the railway has made accessible parts of the Lake District 'previously little visited', and in providing a wealth of tourist information also recognises the potential for taking walks – an ascent of Loughrigg is 'easily ascended from Red Bank', while 'a walk by the side of Nab Scar to Rydal Mount should not be omitted'.

Not until the 20th century did guidebooks for walkers first appear. Symonds' *Walking in the Lake District,* was significant in recognising the need for advice over and above mere description, and includes erudite comments of a practical nature: 'In bog, learn to recognise the moss which lets you in thigh deep'; 'Remember that your balance on steep places is very different with and without a rucksack'. His book also contained 'A few hints on walking'. Curiously, as to what you should take in your rucksack, Symmonds advises that you 'consult a hiker'. Clearly, in his mind there is a distinction between the 'walkers' to whom he is giving advice, and another breed of walker known as 'hiker', but the distinction is not explained, and is far from clear.

Although there continued to be a growing number of books about the Lake District, specifically books recounting exploits among the mountains, notably those of the late Harry Griffin, it was not until 1955 that the first practical guide appeared. Between 1955 and 1966, Kendal Borough Treasurer, Alfred Wainwright, penned seven guidebooks depicting routes up the Lakeland fells. Although still in print, these have long been superseded by guidebooks by contemporary authors, the present author's own two-volume *The Lake Mountains,* appearing in 1987, with many more subsequently.

The present volume is a selection of routes based on 40 years' of walking in the Lake District. They have been included to give a balanced range of walks across the whole National Park and feature the less well-known as well as the popular areas. Walk each route and you will be well on your way to appreciating what the Lake District has to offer.

This book includes a list of waypoints alongside the description of the walk, so that you can enjoy the full benefits of gps should you wish to. For more information on using your gps, read the *Pathfinder® Guide GPS for Walkers*, by gps teacher and navigation trainer, Clive Thomas (ISBN 978-0-7117-4445-5). For essential information on map reading and basic navigation, read the *Pathfinder® Guide Map Reading Skills* by outdoor writer, Terry Marsh (ISBN 978-0-7117-4978-8). Both titles are available in bookshops or can be ordered online at www.pathfinderwalks.co.uk

Introduction

Devoke Water

		GPS waypoints
Start	Birker Fell	
Distance	3 miles (5km)	SD 171 977
Height gain	490 feet (150m)	**Ⓐ** SD 162 970
Approximate time	1½ hours	**Ⓑ** SD 152 969
Parking	Roadside parking spaces	
Route terrain	Rugged mountain tops and tracks; *not advised in poor visibility*	
Ordnance Survey maps	Landranger 96 (Barrow-in-Furness & South Lakeland), Explorer OL6 (The English Lakes – South-western area)	

There seems more to this simple walk than there is. The illusion is created by the vastness of the moorland bowl in which Devoke Water reposes, one where the adjacent fells stand back and so give a distorted sense of their height. But the beauty is in the solitude and away-from-it-all-ness, a quality that is a perfect antidote to the bustle of everyday life. Throw in the fact that so few visitors to Lakeland take the trouble to find this lovely tarn, and connoisseurs of peace and quiet will find it in abundance here.

The key to the start is a minor road junction on the Birker Fell road, where a rusting roadside signpost marks the departure of a bridleway, a broad track, racing off in a westerly direction. The track soon passes a gate and then brings Devoke Water into view, on its shores a partially ruined boat house **Ⓐ** to which the track leads.

(This may be a sufficient walk for some, and the shores of the tarn, close by the boat house, a perfect place to take it all in and then retreat. Strong walkers may want to head for the hills that lie to the south of the tarn. The appearance of considerable height and ruggedness is deceptive, but to bring Yoadcastle and White Pike into the equation will add both immeasurably and pleasurably to the day. There is no evident path to start the ascent, but none is needed, and the joy of

navigating through low crags and across the tops is paramount.)

Devoke Water is the largest tarn in the Lake District, almost a mile in length, and one of the highest at 775 feet (236m). There is an outflow from

Linbeck Gill and Water Crag

the tarn at its north-western corner, where Linbeck Gill flows gently for a short distance before plunging down gushing miniature waterfalls and through a stunning, narrow gorge.

From the boat house, the ongoing track round the tarn is generally clear but intermittently boggy. Your objective is a cairn **B** on the western skyline beyond the end of the lake. It is difficult to imagine it now, but the whole of this area was covered by trees 3,000 years ago. Indeed, the western end of this upland hideaway was peopled in Bronze Age times, as more than 400 hut circles, cairns, enclosures and ancient field systems testify. Tempting though it is to lay at the door of the Scandinavian settlers the blame for the deforestation of the Lake District, that would not be entirely fair. Certainly, the Vikings cleared large tracts of forest, but the rot started when Bronze Age Man stopped living as a nomadic hunter-gatherer and became a settled farmer in need of space in which to plant crops.

A clear path leads up to the cairn, on which there is a low windbreak shelter. From here, the route crosses Linbeck Gill, and generally this is not a problem, although it is easier to cross nearer the

outflow from the tarn than it is farther west once the water has started on its turbulent dash through the Linbeck gorge. If the beck is in spate, it may be wiser to backtrack than to attempt a potentially hazardous leap of faith.

Once beyond the beck, a clear grassy path climbs on to Water Crag, which proves a lovely vantage point, and a good place to seek out a cranny in which to take a break. The top is surmounted by a large cairn, but there is higher ground, an outcrop of red granite, a little to the north.

From Water Crag, a continuing grassy path leads across to Rough Crag, another fine fell with a view out across the windswept grasslands of Birker Fell, and far to the north east and the heart of Lakeland, where the Scafells rule the roost.

One more minor top awaits: Pike How almost overlooks the starting point on the Birker Fell road, and its conquest, a simple grassy plod, will faze no one. From there it is literally downhill all the way across tussocky terrain to rejoin the road.

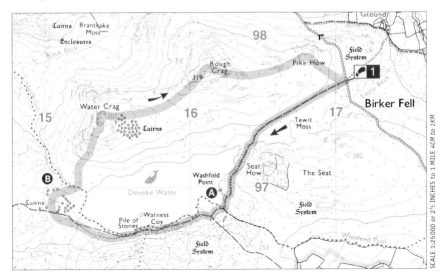

Sweden Bridges

Start	Ambleside market cross	**GPS waypoints**	
Distance	3 miles (5km)	NY 377 045	
Height gain	755 feet (230m)	Ⓐ NY 378 058	
Approximate time	1½ hours	Ⓑ NY 379 067	
Parking	Ambleside	Ⓒ NY 376 057	
Route terrain	Fell farmland; stony tracks; road walking		
Ordnance Survey maps	Landranger 90 (Penrith & Keswick), Explorer OL7 (The English Lakes –South-eastern area)		

Scandale is a fine, fell-framed valley running north from Ambleside and this short walk gives a hint of how tranquil a retreat the valley is. Culminating at High Sweden Bridge, the walk is deservedly popular at any time of year. The name 'Sweden' is believed to derive from 'swithen', a reference to land cleared by burning. The two bridges visited in this walk are packhorse bridges, an indication that Scandale and the pass at its head were once used as a through-route to Patterdale.

Start the walk from the market cross in Ambleside, and set off up North Road. This is the oldest part of the town, known as Ambleside above Stock, and it is here that the town developed as industry grew. Later, after the railway came to Windermere in 1847, tourists came to stay, brought here on stagecoaches operated by the Rigg family who then managed the Windermere Hotel.

When you reach the top of Smithy Brow, near the **Golden Rule** inn, keep forward into Kirkstone Road, and shortly turn left into Sweden Bridge Lane. Keep going up the lane, which becomes increasingly narrow and leads to a gate giving onto an enclosed track. The track climbs steadily between walls, and when it forks, at a gate, bear left.

The track wanders

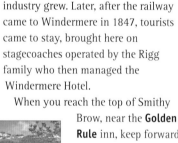

High Sweden Bridge

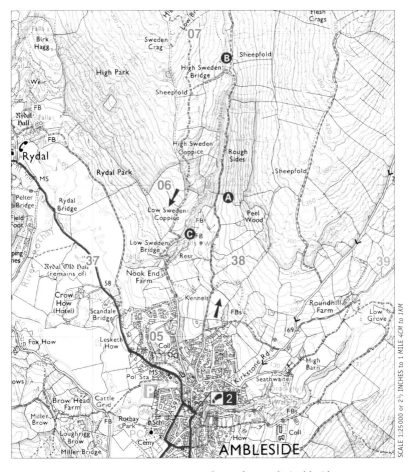

SCALE 1:25000 or 2½ INCHES to 1 MILE 4CM to 1KM

0	200	400	600	800 METRES	1	
						KILOMETRES
						MILES
0	200	400	600 YARDS		½	

upwards at a gentle gradient, with numerous fine views of the Fairfield Horseshoe, and eventually leads into an area of mixed woodland **A**. The ascending track finally breaks free of the woodland and just a short way farther you need to bear left, leaving the Scandale valley track as it reaches High Sweden Bridge **B**.

Cross the bridge and, through the gate on the other side, turn left and follow an ascending path that soon climbs beside a wall to a ladder-stile. After the stile, the path leads off to the left to locate a gap in a wall beyond which a broad grassy track starts to descend towards Ambleside.

The track scampers delightfully down the southern end of the Low Pike ridge towards Ambleside, with views down the length of Windermere. Eventually the path curves round to a gate at a wall corner **C**. Now it continues the descent with good views to the right of the Langdale Pikes, Bowfell, Crinkle Crags and the Coniston Fells.

The track soon makes a loop to cross Low Sweden Bridge. Walk up to Nook End Farm and pass through the farmyard. Beyond, now simply follow a surfaced lane (Nook Lane), back to Ambleside. At the end of Nook Lane, turn right and walk down to the main road and there turn left, following the road to complete the walk. ●

Loughrigg Tarn and the Brathay

		GPS waypoints
Start	Silverthwaite	📝 NY 341 037
Distance	3 miles (4.6km)	Ⓐ NY 341 042
Height gain	525 feet (160m)	Ⓑ NY 345 046
Approximate time	1½ hours	Ⓒ NY 346 040
Parking	At start	Ⓓ NY 343 035
Route terrain	Narrow paths through bracken; rough tracks; country lanes	
Ordnance Survey maps	Landranger 90 (Penrith & Keswick), Explorer OL7 (The English Lakes – South-eastern area)	

Loughrigg Tarn sits like a jewel in a neat hollow below Loughrigg Fell. Its circuit, which is quite delightful, can be made easily by driving up to Tarn Foot, but here the walk is extended to include a stroll along the River Brathay and a visit to Skelwith Force.

📝 Locate the narrow path at the western end of the car park and follow this up alongside the garden wall of Silverthwaite Cottage, climbing steeply at first, but with lovely views of the Langdale Pikes to enliven the way. At a cross-path, keep forward along an obvious route across the shoulder of Little Loughrigg to arrive at a cottage (Crag Head) Ⓐ, and here gain your first view of Loughrigg Tarn.

Loughrigg Tarn was a favoured place of Wordsworth, who, in his *Epistle to Sir George Howland Beaumont Bart,* likened it to 'Diana's Looking-glass ... round clear and bright as heaven', a reference to Lake Nemi, the mirror of Diana in Rome.

Descend to the left of the cottage, and then immediately bear left onto a vehicle access track that leads out to a surfaced lane. Turn left and walk along the road for 175 yds, and then leave it at a signpost by entering a sloping

pasture on the right. Head down field on a grassy path to a stile, and beyond this go forward, taking the higher of two green paths to a gate giving onto a rough track Ⓑ.

Go through the gate and turn right to follow the track to a gate beside a cottage. Press on, and when the ongoing track forks, branch right, past Dillygarth Cottage and soon reach a surfaced lane. Turn left, descending to a road junction, and there turn right, soon crossing a stream near another road junction Ⓒ.

Bear right and follow the road until, near the top of a rise, you can leave it by turning left onto the rough track (now signposted to Skelwith Bridge) to Crag Head used in the earlier part of the walk.

At Crag Head keep forward, following a path through bracken-clad hummocks dotted with low outcrops until you reach a gate giving into the larch woodland of Neaum Crag. Now a gravel path leads forward to the edge of a holiday park of wooden chalets.

Go forward, descending the service road, following a route waymarked by yellow arrows. At a junction, go forward again but immediately after a sleeping policeman across the road, keep to the right of a chalet called 'Angle Tarn'. Pass another – 'Yew Tree Tarn' – and head for a waymarked path enclosed by a low fence. The path leads to a gate. Go left on a path sandwiched between a wall and a fence, which eventually gives into an open field. Keep forward, descending, and head for a kissing-gate giving on to the main road **D**.

Through the gate, turn left and cross the road, turning right at the nearby junction. Very soon, just before Skelwith Bridge, turn right again, now alongside the River Brathay, heading for the Kirkstone Galleries. At the entrance to the galleries, bear right and walk past the workshops and onto a riverside path beyond.

The Brathay is quite a river. If you trace its line back westwards it will lead to a source close by the Three Shire Stone on Wrynose Pass. On its journey,

it first encounters Little Langdale Tarn, quite a gem in itself, has a few flashy flurries in the shape of Colwith Force before changing direction and heading north to feed into Elter Water, where it joins forces with Great Langdale Beck. Flowing east, the river then has another attempt at waterfalls in the shape of Skelwith Force, but this modest descent simply speeds the river up rather than shows off. Even so, it can be quite exciting when in spate, and *not a place to let children loose*.

Pass Skelwith Force, and walk on to a gate giving into a large and flat pasture. Stick to the main path, which courts the river and gradually circles round to draw level with a small knoll crowned by a stand of trees. Leave the main path here by turning right onto a narrow path passing to the right of the knoll, and continuing to a gate giving into woodland.

A gravel path now leads up through trees to the valley road, emerging from cover at a tricky crossing point directly opposite the Silverthwaite car park. *Take care crossing the road.*

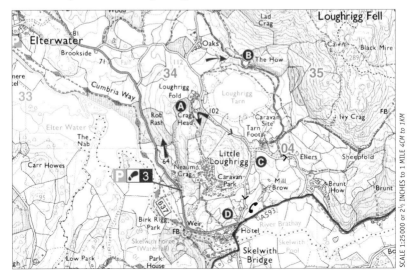

Cat Bells

		GPS waypoints
Start	Hawse End	
Distance	3½ miles (5.6km)	✏ NY 247 212
Height gain	1,150 feet (350m)	**Ⓐ** NY 244 205
		Ⓑ NY 244 192
Approximate time	2 hours	**Ⓒ** NY 248 187
Parking	Hawse End	
Route terrain	Steep ascent and descent through grass and low rock outcrops	
Ordnance Survey maps	Landranger 90 (Penrith & Keswick), Explorer OL4 (The English Lakes – North-western area)	

The distinctive shape of Cat Bells is almost iconic, rising above Derwent Water. Essentially, Cat Bells is the northern extremity of a long ridge that flanks the western side of Borrowdale, and the walk is often used to link with the higher, southern end of the ridge to give a more extensive day on the fells. Here, it is offered as a short walk, but not one that can be taken lightly; the ridge is quite exposed to the elements.

✏ The ascent from Hawse End begins by a stepped path rising up the fellside just south of the hairpin bend on the road from Swinside. Take to the path, enjoying frequent breathers to take in the scenery, and climb steadily

On the summit of Cat Bells

through grass and bracken to tackle a scatter of low rocky outcrops before arriving at the lower, northernmost summit of the fell, which goes by the name Brandelhow **Ⓐ**.

Continue south along the ridge, following a broad trail up the centre of the ridge, before rising quite suddenly and dramatically through more outcrops of rock to the shapely cone of Cat Bells. As is often the case, the final assault on the summit is not so daunting as it appears when viewed end-on.

From the airy viewpoint, you take in the green and blue of Derwent Water, with the ribbed bulk of Blencathra rising in the distance to the north east. More to the north, the sleek sides of Skiddaw rise smoothly above the town of Keswick. To the west, the view is across the Newlands Valley to the high fells above Buttermere – Dalehead, Hindscarth and Robinson, with the Coledale

Horseshoe, culminating in Grisedale Pike a little farther to the north.

To continue the walk, press on across the top of Cat Bells, and now steadily descend to an obvious and wide col, Hause Gate **B**. Here, the route turns left, descending a constructed path, high above the wooded confines of Manesty below. Stay with the descending path until you meet a broad track going left (north) **C**. There are two higher pathways that lead down to this track, but *they can be slippery when wet.*

On reaching the track, turn left and follow it above woodlands that surround Brackenburn Lodge, sometime home of New Zealand-born novelist Hugh Walpole (1884–1941), best remembered these days for his series of books *The Herries Chronicles,* set in and around Borrowdale. Walpole lies buried in St John's churchyard in Keswick.

Keep following the path northwards, past Brackenburn, beyond which it descends to make a brief encounter with a surfaced lane at a small, disused quarry. A short way farther on, you return to a gently rising path across the lower slopes of Cat Bells, and this eventually returns you to Hawse End. There, cross the road and go down a shortcut to a gate near a cattle-grid, from which you soon reach the start of the walk. ●

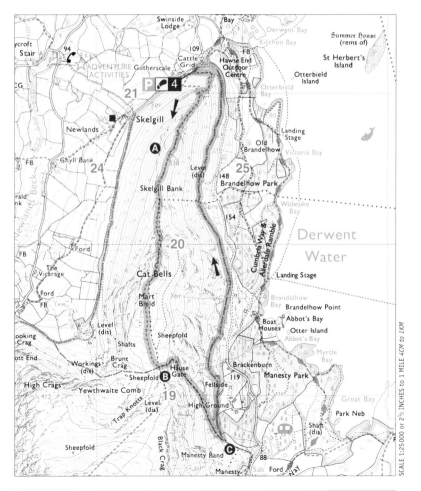

Buttermere

		GPS waypoints
Start	Buttermere	NY 173 169
Distance	4½ miles (7km)	**Ⓐ** NY 172 163
Height gain	395 feet (120m)	**Ⓑ** NY 189 147
Approximate time	2 hours	**Ⓒ** NY 189 156
Parking	Buttermere village	
Route terrain	Good paths throughout; some road walking	
Ordnance Survey maps	Landranger 90 (Penrith & Keswick), Explorer OL4 (The English Lakes – North-western area)	

There is no finer, or simpler, lake circuit than this delightful tour of Buttermere. You are surrounded by high fells which are a marvellous backdrop, and there is delight at every step of the way. Strong walkers can combine this circuit with an ascent of Hay Stacks (Walk 13) to give a longer day.

Leaving from Buttermere, exit the car park and turn down the track past the **Fish Hotel**, one of the oldest hostelries in the Lake District, and immortalised in Lakeland history by the many and varied tales of the Maid of Buttermere. The track leads to the edge of the lake (ignore the turning to Scale Force), and then follows the line of a hedgerow to Buttermere Dubs, a narrow waterway linking to nearby Crummock Water.

Cross a footbridge Ⓐ and go through a gate at the foot of Burtness Wood, to

Buttermere village and Grasmoor

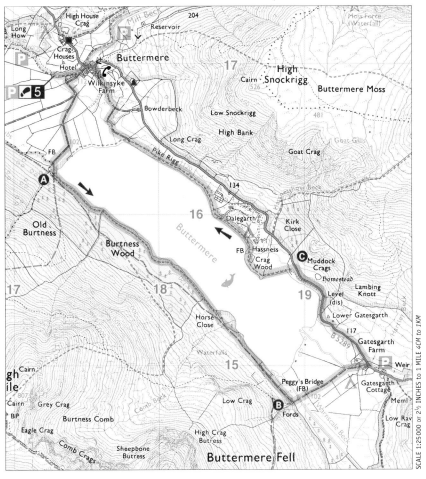

begin a long and delightful route close by the edge of Buttermere lake. The route finally reaches Horse Close, where a bridge spans Comb Beck. Continue along the path to reach a wall leading to a sheepfold and gate **B**.

Bear left through the gate to descend to and cross Peggy's Bridge spanning Warnscale Beck, and then follow a clear path out to meet the valley road at Gatesgarth Farm. From the farm you turn left along the road – take care against approaching traffic. As the road bends left, leave it for a footpath on the left for the Lakeshore Path **C**, which

leads into a field, and presses on to Crag Wood, never far from the shoreline. The route leads you into the grounds of Hassness, a fine mansion once owned by a Manchester mill owner, George Benson. At one point the route lies through a tunnel, cut by Benson's employees so that the man could walk around the lake without having to get too far from it.

After the tunnel, a gate gives on to a gravel path through a wooded pasture, after which a right turn onto a fenced path leads to a bridge of slate slabs. Eventually a path guides you up to Wilkinsyke Farm, and an easy stroll out to the road. Turn left to return to the starting point. ●

Dalemain and Dacre

			GPS waypoints
Start	Dalemain		🖊 NY 477 270
Distance	4½ miles (7.25km)		Ⓐ NY 471 257
Height gain	445 feet (135m)		Ⓑ NY 471 249
Approximate time	2 hours		Ⓒ NY 464 254
Parking	Dalemain		Ⓓ NY 459 265
Route terrain	Farmland; some road walking; woodland		
Ordnance Survey maps	Landranger 90 (Penrith & Keswick), Explorer OL5 (The English Lakes – North-eastern area)		

With the kind permission of the owners, this walk begins from Dalemain, heading from there towards Dunmallard Hill, and then skipping across fields to the village of Dacre. It is a short walk, but one laden with an unprecedented amount of history, antiquity and intrigue.

🖊 Set off from the car park at Dalemain and follow the main drive out to the road. There turn right, following the road briefly as it crosses Dacre Beck just west of its confluence with the River Eamont. Leave the road at a stile just south of the Dacre Bridge to enter a large pasture.

Dalemain is a largely 18th-century mansion built around an earlier manor and, possibly, a pele tower believed to date from Norman times. The property has remained in the same family since 1680, when Sir Edward Hasell, the son of the rector of Middleton Cheney in Northamptonshire, purchased it from the de Laytons. Sir Edward was secretary to Lady Anne Clifford until her death in 1675, when he settled in Cumberland. He married Jane Fetherstonhaugh of Kirkoswald, and, after sitting as Member of Parliament for Cumberland, was knighted by William III.

Today the mansion is open to visitors, as are the gardens, which have been developed by succeeding generations to provide five acres of richly planted herbaceous borders. Of particular interest to fatigued walkers is the splendid **tearoom** complete with large open fire.

Bear left across the pasture to connect with a broad grassy track leading up to the top corner of Langfield Wood. As you reach the edge of the woodland, walk across to a waymark and then a gate/stile from which you follow a grassy track alongside a fence, directly targeting Dunmallard Hill.

The fenceside path eventually leads down to intercept another at which you can turn left and walk out to the A592 Ⓐ. Cross the road to a verge opposite and turn left. After about 50 yds, turn through a kissing-gate giving on to a footpath for Pooley Bridge. Now walk along the edge of a large field, with a fence on your left.

Soon, the path passes a small lake fringed with bulrush, and runs on along a line of beautiful Lombardy poplar trees. Lombardy poplar trees, which have distinctive upturned branches that form a towering spire, were once regularly planted to adorn driveways and to act as wind breaks. One childhood tale relates that the poplar furls its branches upwards because it was within them that King Charles II sought to escape the Roundheads at the end of the English Civil War in 1651. Of course, that could not have been possible, however delightful a notion, because the Lombardy poplar was not introduced into Britain until 1758 by Lord Rochford, then ambassador to Turin. Tradition has it that it was an oak tree in the grounds of Boscobel House on the border of Shropshire that actually sheltered the fugitive king.

At the end of the line of poplars, cross a step-stile and walk around the end of the lake to a gate in a badly drained corner close by the River Eamont. Now simply parallel the river, heading upstream, with the path crossing the base of a number of fields before reaching a gate **B** entering a field below wooded Dunmallard Hill.

Through the gate turn right, climbing beside a fence until, higher up, you can cross it at a step-stile, and keep alongside it once more until it descends to meet the A592.

Cross the road and go through a gate opposite, and then follow a fence on the left. The fenceside path crosses two fields and eventually climbs to a gate and stile at a narrow lane, adjoining a monumental sycamore tree **C**. Turn right and stroll along the lane to a road

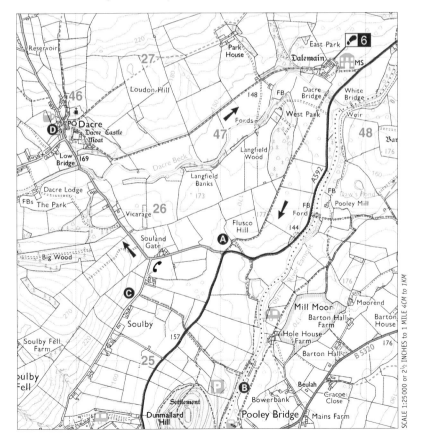

junction, and there turn left walking easily towards the village of Dacre.

As you crest a rise, so Dacre comes into view. A long descent leads down to the village. Cross Dacre Beck and walk uphill to the tiny village green complete with stocks. Opposite this, turn right onto a path **D** that leads to Dacre Castle. However, it is first worth continuing up the road to visit the church. The Church of St Andrew has a Norman west tower and a late 12th-century chancel, and is believed to have been built on the site of the Saxon monastery mentioned by the Venerable Bede in his Ecclesiastical History of 731, as being 'built near the River Dacre'.

Also of interest in the church is the lock on the south door. It is dated 1671, and is one of a number of locks presented by Lady Anne Clifford to those who had shown her particular kindness. The locks were made for Lady Anne by George Dent of Appleby, and cost £1 each.

The church also contains a memorial tablet to Edward Hasell, bearing a kneeling female figure, which is believed to be the only work in the county of Sir Francis Legatt Chantrey (1781-1841), Derbyshire-born English sculptor, famed for his portrait statues and busts.

Of particular intrigue, at the corners of the churchyard stand the enigmatic Dacre Bears, four large sculptures cut in stone, now well weathered, and thought to commemorate the marriage between Thomas de Dacre and Philippa Neville, although their true origin is unknown. The monuments seem to depict an encounter between a bear and a cat: one shows the bear sleeping, then the cat awakens the bear, which seizes the cat, kills it and promptly eats it.

Return to the village green and take the path that leads past Dacre Castle. Like most Cumberland castles, Dacre Castle began life as a pele tower, and was built in the 14th century. In 1354, a licence for a chapel in the castle was granted by Bishop Welton of Carlisle, and a new tower was added in 1485. It was completely renovated by the last Lord Dacre, Earl of Sussex, in the 1680s and in 1716 it was sold to Sir Christopher Musgrave, who in turn transferred it to his son-in-law Edward Hasell of Dalemain. In times of trouble, villagers would take refuge in Dacre Castle, which would have afforded considerable security, with its massive walls and battlements.

Press on past the castle, following a broad farm track that leads across large pastures and becomes a simple stroll that feeds you in to the rear of Dalemain. Turn left through the archway to return to the car park, although a post perambulatory pot of tea and buttered scones may give you time to digest all the history blended into this walk. ●

Dalemain

Ravenglass and Muncaster

		GPS waypoints
Start	Ravenglass	
Distance	4½ miles (7km)	🔖 SD 085 964
Height gain	670 feet (210m)	**Ⓐ** SD 093 957
		Ⓑ SD 099 960
Approximate time	2 hours	**Ⓒ** SD 099 969
Parking	Free parking in Ravenglass	**Ⓓ** SD 097 976
Route terrain	Woodland; farmland; managed parkland	**Ⓔ** SD 093 966
Ordnance Survey maps	Landranger 96 (Barrow-in-Furness & South Lakeland), Explorer OL6 (The English Lakes – South-western area)	

A view across a lovely estuary, where three rivers have their confluence, is Ravenglass's outlook on the world: a shingle beach, a few small yachts waiting companionably for the tide, and a steady trade in birdlife. This one-street village, the only coastal village within the Lake District National Park, was granted a market charter as long ago as the 13th century, and has a history to match. From it, this walk ventures inland to the privately owned Muncaster Castle, before taking an extra dip into local history by visiting the Muncaster Mill on the banks of the River Mite.

🔖 Set off from the car park, passing between buildings to turn left along the village street – there is only one to choose from – and at its end, bear left to locate a passageway beneath the railway line. Cross a narrow lane beyond, and then turn right on a footpath that leads directly to the Bath House that once served the Roman fort of Glannoventa.

There are substantial remains of the bath house, although without the nearby interpretation panel it is difficult to make much sense of the layout. The site of the fort, of which only earthen shapes remain, was largely on the opposite side of the narrow lane, and part was destroyed when the railway was constructed.

From the 1st to the 3rd century CE, more than 1,000 soldiers occupied the fort at Ravenglass, which served as a vital command and supply centre for the Roman occupation of the north-western part of England. Some authorities conjecture that Ravenglass was the southernmost of a string of Roman coastal defences around Cumbria, extending south from Hadrian's Wall; others suggest that the fort was not known as Glannoventa at all, but rather Itunocelum.

Keep on past the bath house, and when the roadside path ends, bear left onto a broad track that leads up to Newtown House. Ignore the first path for Muncaster branching on the left, and keep on until level with the buildings, when you can take either a gate on the left or walk a few strides farther to a signposted footpath **Ⓐ**. Both combine almost instantly, but then divide again. Take the right branch, following a path that plunges you into the murkiness of a dense conifer plantation. Mercifully, this is relatively short-lived, and before long you shake off the trees to clamber over a stile into a large pasture, a former deer park belonging to Muncaster Castle. Now continue in a north-easterly direction, keeping to the right of a low rocky knoll on the left, but without any discernible footpath to confirm the direction.

Maintain the same direction, and as you cross the pasture so a distant wall comes into view, and then a signpost, which pinpoints the location of a gate **B** giving into the grounds of Muncaster Castle. A delightful path then leads through bluebell woodland, and on beneath a wide range of exotic trees and shrubs. When the path forks, branch right to see a view of the castle that now appears below. The path gradually descends to intercept a broad track.

The path just travelled is a right of way through the grounds, and it continues now across a grassy area towards the Stables Yard ahead. Walk up a surfaced lane to the left of the Stables Yard and soon you will reach the church, and then walk out to meet the A595.

With the exception of the facility to use **toilets** *(opposite the plant centre gates, near the church) and the purchase of light refreshments from the* **Owl Garden Tea Room***, it is important to realise that the ability to walk along the right of way does not carry with it the right to leave it and explore the castle grounds (for which you need a 'Walker's Ticket', available only to those arriving at Muncaster by public footpaths).*

Muncaster Castle *(see page 95 for details)* is the ancient seat of the Pennington family, a lineage that has survived for more than 800 years thanks, it is said, to the ongoing survival intact of a glass drinking bowl – known as the Luck of Muncaster – given to the family by Henry VI with the earnest prayer that the family might prosper so long as the bowl remained unbroken. The regal gesture was in response to hospitality given to the king after he was found wandering the fells following the Battle of Towton in 1461 during the Wars of the Roses (the largest and bloodiest ever fought on British soil), although authorities argue that it may have been after the Battle of Hexham three years later. The glass bowl has remained intact ever since, and its whereabouts are a closely guarded family secret.

On reaching the A595, cross it and turn left, walking to a nearby bend. Go forward, leaving the road, onto a farm access track that leads to Branken Wall Farm. Walk as far as a gate **C** on the right, opposite the end of a track arriving from the left. Turn right through the gate into woodland, and follow the ongoing track until it divides into three. Take either the middle or the

The remains of Roman Bath House, Ravenglass

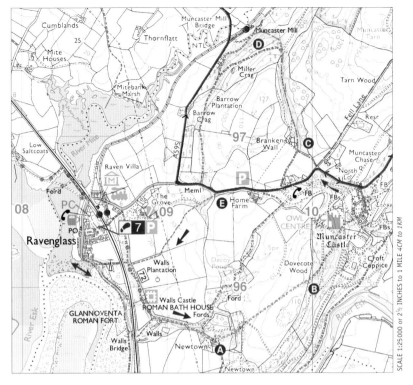

left track. The former takes you down to a broad track behind Muncaster Mill; the latter effects a shortcut.

Muncaster Mill (not open to the public) is a water-powered mill dating from 1455. The present building, however, dates from the early 18th century, and electricity was generated by the mill until 1958, using a waterwheel. It is possible that the Romans may have used the mill, or at least the site of it, as the Mite is tidal to this point. The mill was part of the Pennington Estate until 1970.

If you took the path down to the mill, then on reaching the broad track, you need to turn left, but to take the higher of two tracks, a path for Ravenglass, rising on the left **D**. This crosses poorly drained ground and is often muddy in places. The path rises to meet a path from the left, which is the alternative path used by those taking the shortcut mentioned above.

Now continue climbing gently to leave the woodland at a gate, after which the track continues ascending across a gorsey landscape above the estuary of the River Mite. Eventually, the route emerges on the A595. Cross the road and turn left, walking for about 100 yds, and then leaving the road for a footpath on the right **E**, leading into light woodland.

You leave the woodland at a kissing-gate, from which you strike across rough pasture in a south-westerly direction, following a grassy path to a gate in a mid-field fence. Through the gate, turn right alongside the fence and follow it out to meet the narrow lane and path used earlier in the walk. Now go forward across the lane and under the railway line to return to Ravenglass and complete the walk. ●

Little Mell Fell

Start	Thackthwaite	GPS waypoints
Distance	4¼ miles (6.75km)	⬢ NY 417 252
Height gain	1,065 feet (325m)	Ⓐ NY 414 241
Approximate time	2½ hours	Ⓑ NY 416 246
		Ⓒ NY 429 238
Parking	Limited roadside parking along minor road	
Route terrain	Country lanes; open, grassy fellside	
Ordnance Survey maps	Landranger 90 (Penrith & Keswick), Explorer OL5 (The English Lakes – North-eastern area)	

The difficulties of finding somewhere safe and convenient to park should deter no one from tackling this exquisite little walk. With its slightly higher neighbour, Great Mell Fell, Little Mell Fell sits placidly to the south of the A66. This is uncomplicated walking – enjoyable, breathtaking and refreshing.

🖊 The lane that runs to the south of Thackthwaite does provide a few roadside indentations in which to park, and from wherever that might be, set off in a westerly direction. Wood sorrel in the hedgerows tells of a time when all of this area was wooded. Today it is open and offers lovely views northwards to Carrock Fell and Souther Fell, and ahead to Great Mell Fell. Determined walkers can link the two fells into one long day of the most agreeable fell wandering.

At a junction take the lane on the left, for Lowthwaite. Walking along this road is no hardship, sliding as it does across the western flank of Little Mell Fell high above the infant Dacre Beck, and with distant views of the Dodds and Helvellyn.

Go past the turning for Greenrow and Fox Hill, and finally leave the road, high above Foxhill Farm, for an overgrown vehicle track Ⓐ going up to a gate. Beyond the gate the track climbs a little farther but then swings back on itself, climbing steadily through a rash of gorse. Cross a fence by a stile, and maintain the same direction passing through more gorse, and following an uncertain narrow path. Just as the path starts to descend you can branch right (NY 415 244), continuing to climb through gorse.

Once beyond the gorse, the ascending path broadens into an easy-angled rake, and rises to meet an old field boundary marked by a line of gnarled and twisted hawthorn Ⓑ. Cross the old boundary and climb the slope above, a brief, steep and pathless climb at the top of which the summit of Little Mell Fell hoves into view.

Now turn to head roughly in a southerly direction, up gently rising ground with the faintest suggestion of a path etched into the short, springy turf and moss. Once a fenceline comes into view ahead, backed by the ragged profile of Gowbarrow Fell set against that of Place Fell, bear left, turning now more in the direction of the summit.

As you approach the fence, go left with it, and this will guide you to a fence corner where you can step over a fence from which barbs have been removed to enable you to do so. From the corner, head across an upland pasture towards a gate in another fence.

Once beyond the gate, simply follow a grassy path up on to the top of the fell,

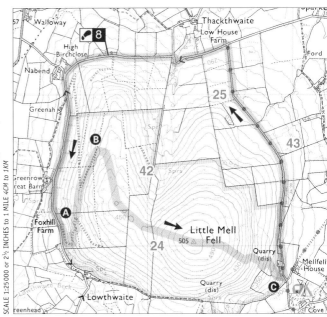

SCALE 1:25000 or 2½ INCHES to 1 MILE 4CM to 1KM

which is marked by a trig pillar. The geology of Little and Great Mell Fells is interesting as Carboniferous rocks form a conglomerate in which pebbles are set in a sandy matrix. Unusually the pebbles come from Skiddaw slate, Borrowdale Volcanic rocks, Coniston limestone, Silurian grit and even Shap granite. The assumption is that in the distant past they were carried to the Mell Fell site by powerful floods and resistant to erosion they now form the smooth, rounded fells visible today.

The popular line of ascent comes up from the south, but this walk continues across the summit in an easterly direction, towards what little you can just see of Ullswater. Before long the descent steepens as it heads down towards Mellfell House caravan park. After a while, the descending path peters out and you are left to determine your own way down through bracken.

As you descend, once you can locate an isolated house at the foot of the fell, this helps because now you can head towards it, and along the way you will intercept a lateral path. You have the

choice of continuing the direct descent, but it is easier to turn left along the lateral path, descending gently until you can drop down to the right to a fence corner, next to a stream running down a gully.

Turn right, away from the fence corner, and follow the stream. When you reach a fence, where the stream changes direction, turn left. Had you made the direct descent, this is the point you would have been aiming for. Walk down beside a fence to a gate, and then by gates descend to meet a surfaced lane **C**.

On reaching the lane, turn immediately left – it's the first of two lanes on the left, climbing gently and proving to be a splendid track streaking northwards, a delight to follow with far-reaching views eastwards to Cross Fell, and north to Carrock Fell and Bowscale.

Eventually, the track descends to intercept the Thackthwaite road. Here, turn left and follow the road back to your starting point.

Loweswater

		GPS waypoints
Start	Loweswater	NY 135 210
Distance	5½ miles (8.6km)	Ⓐ NY 124 201
Height gain	885 feet (270m)	Ⓑ NY 107 225
Approximate time	2½ hours	Ⓒ NY 118 218
Parking	Maggie's Bridge	
Route terrain	Farmland, fell slopes, woodland trails and lakeshore paths	
Ordnance Survey maps	Landranger 89 (West Cumbria), Explorer OL4 (The English Lakes – North-western area)	

This pleasing walk makes use of a terraced path across the lower slopes of Burnbank Fell, and once free of the woodland screen that is Holme Wood, provides a terrific prospect of Loweswater slotted neatly into a hollow below Darling Fell and Low Fell. The walk can be followed easily in either direction.

Leave the car park, walking to the left and then immediately to the right to cross Maggie's Bridge, which spans Dub Beck. Now follow a broad track across fields in the company of High Nook Beck to reach High Nook

Loweswater

Farm. Bear right through the farmyard, to gain a rough track on the other side climbing above High Nook Beck.

The track climbs to a gate in a wall, beyond which, a short way farther on, just as the track forks, branch right descending slightly. Just after the path starts to descend a little more, leave and

bear right across marshy ground to a footbridge  *(A short, optional extension, but one well worth it on a sunny day, is to keep heading in a south-westerly direction instead of crossing the marshy ground, and you will soon reach the lovely confines of High Nook Tarn, tucked out of sight.)*

Over the footbridge, bear right on an ascending track to reach the southern edge of Holme Wood. As it reaches the boundary wall of the mixed woodland the track levels, although it does climb again a short way farther on, rising to a gate and stile after which it heads downhill with Loweswater now appearing through the pines on the right. Ahead the view extends to the estuary of Solway Firth and the distant hills of Galloway in southern Scotland.

The path eventually leaves the woodland edge and turns inland to cross Holme Beck by a wide footbridge. The ongoing track then undulates, and passes a memorial chair to Roy Farrell. While it is tempting to think this may be the Roy Farrell who co-founded Cathay Pacific Airways, it is highly unlikely, and in any case irrelevant – it's the view that matters, and that is outstanding.

Continue past the chair, now climbing steadily to a gate in a wall

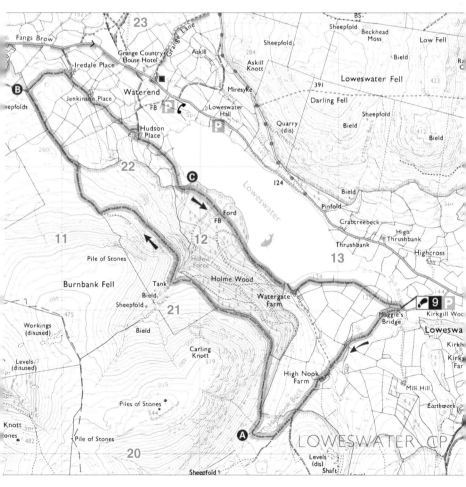

corner. Through the gate, continue alongside the wall and keep following the track until about 200 yds before reaching the road at Fangs Brow, you can leave the track for a bridleway on the right **B**, passing through two gates and then taking a clear route downhill to arrive at Iredale Place.

When the descending track intercepts another, keep forward and soon reach Jenkinson Place. Here again, keep forward, now with Loweswater fully in view, and press on towards Hudson's Place, and soon passing through a field gate and following a grassy track as it slopes obliquely down to another gate. Beyond, the track is less distinct, but follows an old field boundary marked by mature hawthorns. Just as you approach Hudson's Place, go left at a gate/stile and follow a wall, walking out to meet a surfaced lane.

Turn right, and follow the lane past Hudson's Place and then bear left through a gate onto a broad, enclosed footpath leading down towards the lake. After passing through another gate, the ongoing track takes a lovely route along the edge of the lake, and then eventually enters Holme Wood **C**, a National Trust property, through which a stony track threads an agreeable way.

Holme Wood was planted between 1945 and 1955 using Sitka and Norway spruce, and it stands on the site of an ancient oak woodland. The pines close to the track are mainly Scots pine. During 1994, large areas of spruce were cleared and replanted with sessile oak and larch in an effort to restore the woodland to its former glory.

Once free of the woodland, you soon reach Watergate Farm. As you do so, turn immediately left and follow a service track initially beside the lake, and then continuing back to Maggie's Bridge. ●

Loweswater Fell from the track to High Nook Farm

Glenridding and Lanty's Tarn

		GPS waypoints	
Start	Glenridding		NY 386 169
Distance	5¼ miles (8.3km)	**Ⓐ**	NY 379 169
Height gain	1,015 feet (310m)	**Ⓑ**	NY 363 173
Approximate time	2½ hours	**Ⓒ**	NY 376 167
Parking	Glenridding (Pay and Display)	**Ⓓ**	NY 381 159
Route terrain	Stony tracks; some road walking; open fellside		
Ordnance Survey maps	Landranger 90 (Penrith & Keswick), Explorer OL5 (The English Lakes – North-eastern area)		

The renown of Glenridding as one of the key tourist hotspots of the Lake District is far reaching. From here walkers launch themselves into the hills, while less energetic moments can be spent along the lakeshore or taking to one of the steamers that regularly ply up and down the lake. This was once a major mining area, and a veritable hive of industrial activity in years gone by. Taking the opportunity to visit the mining area, this walk then slips southwards into neighbouring Grisedale by way of secluded Lanty's Tarn, a spot quiet enough to attract goosander at some times of year.

Leave the main car park by walking out to the road and turning right to cross Glenridding Bridge, and then immediately right onto a narrow lane for Miresbeck and Helvellyn. Walk past a whitewashed cottage with circular chimneys typical of the Lake District, and probably dating from the late 18th century. Beyond this the lane becomes a stony track. When it forks, branch right and go towards Glenridding Beck, now following a lovely track around a camp site to emerge onto a surfaced lane at Gillside.

Turn right and cross Rattlebeck Bridge **Ⓐ**. The on-going lane comes out at a wider road. Go left, climbing gently and when, shortly, it forks, keep left

again for Greenside Mine and Sticks Pass, to pass below rows of terraced cottages that once served the miners and their families.

The fells on your right (north) are Glenridding Dodd and Sheffield Pike *(see Walk 14)*, while to the south looms the massive bulk of Birkhouse Moor. The ongoing track is most agreeable and ambles up towards the main mining site. Lead ore was first discovered at what became the Greenside Lead Mine in the 1650s, the first levels being driven by Dutch adventurers in the 1690s, and dressed ore was carried to the Stoneycroft smelter at Keswick. Production at the mine, however, did not really begin until the late 18th

Eagle Cottage, Glenridding

century, and the mine was not extensively worked until 1825, when mining activity reached its height following the setting up of the Greenside Mining Company in 1822. Power was originally provided by waterwheels, with the water being supplied by the damming of nearby tarns. One of them, Keppel Cove, burst its banks on October 29, 1927, bringing disaster to the village below. Much the same happened four years later, when flood waters smashed through the concrete of High Dam.

At the height of its activity, the Greenside Mine was not only the largest lead mine in the Lake District, with over 300 employees, but was also a pioneer, being the first to use electricity to power the winding gear, and it also ran the first underground electric engine in British ore mines.

By the early 1960s it had become uneconomic to continue to extract lead from the mine, and it closed, the last ore being extracted in April 1961. But that was not entirely the end of the story for the mine was then used to test instruments designed to detect underground nuclear explosions. Most of the mine buildings are now gone, but a few remain and see service as a youth

hostel and mountain huts; in fact, a bridge seat at Swart Beck is a perfect place to take a breather.

Follow the path as it ascends past the youth hostel, crosses Swart Beck and then by a waymarked route threads a group of buildings to take a waymarked track for Red Tarn and Helvellyn, straight ahead. The path climbs to a footbridge **B** spanning the upper reaches of Glenridding Beck, here flowing down from Keppel Cove.

Over the bridge turn left and take to the course of an old leat, which cuts an almost level path across the slopes of Birkhouse Moor. Another option takes a lower course, running along a woodland boundary and then a wall.

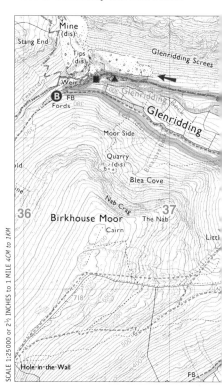

SCALE 1:25000 or 2½ INCHES to 1 MILE 4CM to 1KM

But the leat is of admirable purpose, and much preferred, finally concluding at a low wall that deflects walkers down to the lower path.

Now walk beside a wall to a gate **C**, where you pass onto a descending stony track that comes down to intercept a rough track serving a nearby cottage. Bear right and cross a footbridge, now taking to a path for Grisedale and Lanty's Tarn. Pass through a wall gap and then pursue a waymarked route across rough pasture.

The path leads up to a gate in a wall. Through it bear right, climbing easily and generally towards a seat at the top of the incline. As you crest a rise, Lanty's Tarn comes into view, just beyond a gate. Pass to the right of the tarn, emerging on the other side to a splendid view of Grisedale. Quite who

'Lanty' of Lanty's Tarn was, is unknown; perhaps a smuggler or illicit whisky distiller, both activities being prevalent across the Lake District in the past. The tarn is formed by a low dam, and the probability is that this was done by the Marshalls at Patterdale Hall; reputedly there is an underground cellar below the dam which may well have been used as an ice house, such not being uncommon, although there is no conclusive evidence of this.

As you pass the far end of the tarn, the path drops towards Grisedale, and affords ever-improving views up this delightful valley. Eventually you approach a couple of gates, both of which give on to the track up to Striding Edge. Take the left-hand gate **D** and then turn left down a sloping pasture to a gate at the bottom giving on to a narrow lane. Follow this across Grisedale Beck and out to a T-junction, there turning left to follow a surfaced lane down past Patterdale Hall and out to meet the main valley road.

The hall, not open to the public, is substantially rebuilt, but dates from around 1677.

Turn left at the road and cross to a path opposite, soon branching onto a path through roadside trees. A short way farther on you pop out onto the road again. Cross with care and continue onto a raised footpath on the opposite side, later re-crossing the road for the final stretch back into the centre of Glenridding.

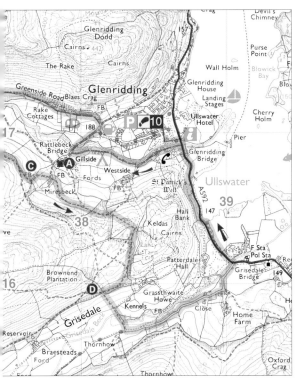

Seathwaite Tarn

		GPS waypoints
Start	Seathwaite	
Distance	4¾ miles (7.6km)	SD 229 962
Height gain	1,065 feet (325m)	Ⓐ SD 240 968
Approximate time	2½ hours	Ⓑ SD 245 982
Parking	Roadside parking near Seathwaite church	Ⓒ SD 237 977
Route terrain	Fell moorland; woodland; farmland; some road walking	
Ordnance Survey maps	Landranger 96 (Barrow-in-Furness & South Lakeland), Explorer OL6 (The English Lakes – South-western area)	

Reposing beneath the steep slopes of Grey Friar near the head of the Duddon Valley, Seathwaite Tarn lies in a most profound location, one with a capacity to absorb a disproportionate amount of time doing nothing. The Duddon Valley itself, known as Dunnerdale, is a little-frequented part of the region as narrow, twisting roads deter visitors. Only the determined and the curious seek out Dunnerdale rewards, and there are many. Seathwaite Tarn is one of them. The walk starts from a parking area beside the River Duddon, just behind the church.

The name Seathwaite derives from a combination of the old Norse words *sef* (sedges) and *thveit* (later anglicised to 'thwaite', meaning a clearing) and may be taken to mean a clearing among the sedges. The name, then written Seuthwayt, first appeared in records dating from 1340.

A notable treasure of Seathwaite, not far from the start of the walk, is the **Newfield Inn**, a pub that dates from the packhorse days of the 16th century, and was visited by Wordsworth on his tours of the Lake District. The pub's most unusual feature is its banded slate floor, a product of the time when slate was easily gained and plentiful.

The Church of the Holy Trinity was built in the early 1500s, but has seen much restoration. Wordsworth visited the church and dedicated one of his *Duddon Sonnets* to the place and to the Reverend Robert Walker (1709-1802) who was parson here for 66 years. The church contains a memorial plaque to Walker, who was known as 'Wonderful Walker' because of his long and exemplary ministry. Wordsworth refers to him in the sonnet as '... a Gospel Teacher ... whose good works formed an endless retinue'. Prior to the inn opening, the Reverend Walker even brewed and sold his own ale.

🖋 Turn left up the road beside the bubbling Duddon, a watercourse of bright turquoise plunge pools and foaming cascades surrounded by trees favoured by red squirrels.

After about 440 yds, leave the road by turning right towards Turner Hall

Farm. As you approach the farm, go forward through a gate for High Moss and follow a broad track around the farm and on across fields to High Moss.

The summits directly in front of you are part of the Dow Crag ridge, extending south to White Maiden; you can pick out the course of the Walna Scar Road crossing the slopes of the fells.

At High Moss, keep to the left of the buildings to locate a gate giving into a rough pasture. Cross this to a narrow lane. Turn right and walk past Beck House; if you look half-left you will now see a slanting rake leading off to the northern skyline. This is the way the route is going.

When you reach a bridge **Ⓐ** spanning Long House Gill, where the Walna Scar Road begins its upward journey, turn left over the bridge onto a superb service track rising at an easy gradient and leading all the way to Seathwaite Tarn. Prominent in view to the left is the pyramidal Harter Fell, and, perhaps less obviously, through a gap in the fells Scafell and Slight Side loom.

Once the track levels, as it nears the tarn, you pass a low waymark on the left **Ⓑ**; note this for the return stage. Continue along the track with the great bulk of Grey Friar now putting in an appearance. The beauty of this approach to the tarn is that you do not see the lake until virtually the last

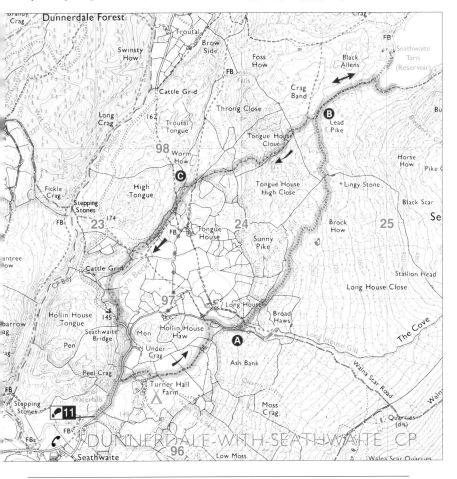

Seathwaite Tarn and Grey Friar

moment, and that is heralded by the appearance of the dam wall. When you arrive at the tarn base, turn up to the right for a lovely view across the water; there is a path all the way round the tarn, but this is often marshy at the far end and a worthy compromise is either to remain near the dam or to walk a little farther to a prominent rise, which proves to be an excellent vantage point.

Seathwaite Tarn was dammed in the 1930s to provide drinking water for Barrow-in-Furness. Its setting in a grand mountain hollow is superb, and the waters of the tarn are deep and shelve quickly.

Return by the upward route, as far as that low waymark, and there branch right on a clear footpath that wanders downwards in a most agreeable fashion through a series of rock outcrops and boulders, and later accompanies a stream, which at some point you need to step across to continue the descent. Eventually, the descent moves away from the stream, but the path is clear throughout and leads down to a gate as it enters the valley bottom. Keep

following the path to another gate, after which you bear right to a ladder-stile, then crossing Tarn Beck by a footbridge **⊙**. On the other side, go half-left to a gate giving onto a path along the base of a wooded slope, and on the true right bank of Tarn Bank, which, alas, soon changes direction.

Keep to the right of a barn and cottage and then continue along the base of wooded slopes and beside a moss-covered wall. Just on passing a long, low barn the track bears off to the right, but keep an eye open for a path bearing left down from the main track to run alongside a fence. You can follow the main track if you wish, and it will lead you out to a road, but this gives you more road walking to complete the walk than necessary. *Instead, keep along the fence to a gate, and then by a path around a marshy area, with a few duckboards in place, and head out to meet a bridge spanning the Duddon.*

Turn left and cross the bridge, and then pass a road turning for Coniston, and farm access lanes to Under Crag and then Turner Hall beyond which you simply stroll down the road to complete the walk. ●

Branstree and Selside Pike

Start	Mardale Head	**GPS waypoints**	
Distance	5½ miles (9.2km)	✏ NY 469 107	
Height gain	1,740 feet (530m)	Ⓐ NY 474 092	
Approximate time	3 hours	Ⓑ NY 494 123	
Parking	Mardale Head		
Route terrain	Moorland fell tops with few distinguishing features		
Ordnance Survey maps	Landranger 90 (Penrith & Keswick), Explorer OL5 (The English Lakes – North-eastern area)		

Most walkers visiting the roadhead at Mardale are bound for the summits around High Street (see Walk 19), or visiting to see if they can spot any remains of the village of Mardale, drowned with the raising of the reservoir in the 1930s, taking with it a way of life so poignantly exemplified by Sarah Hall in her novel Haweswater.
But the heights to the east of the roadhead, those of Mardale Common and Swindale Common, are a real reward for anyone wanting solitude and quiet days. This walk explores less well-known summits, nevertheless well worthy of investigation.

From Mardale the slopes of Branstree, the first summit, are suitable only for walkers with calf muscles like barrage balloons and something to prove. Luckily for lesser mortals, like the author, there is a much more agreeable route.

✏ Leave the roadhead at Mardale and walk through a gate, taking the left-hand stony track that rises steadily, parallel with the boundary of a nearby plantation, but then changing direction below the craggy face of Harter Fell to fashion a splendid ascent never far from the company of Gatescarth Beck.

Gatescarth is the name of the pass to which you are ascending, and it is a walk of pure delight to amble upwards

at a steady plod until you reach a gate and fence across the pass Ⓐ. This was something of a trade route in the past linking two dales. Beyond the pass, the ground falls swiftly into the head of Long Sleddale. It is all remote and wonderful, a glorious mess of crags, becks, walls and mire.

For the moment, on reaching the pass, from where a clear path sets off in a westerly direction onto Harter Fell, simply pass through the gate and turn immediately left beside the fence. Dance around a small boggy patch of ground in a dip, and then engage an easy pull on grass, beside the fence, all the way to the top of Branstree. Cross the fence by a step-stile close by a wall.

The summit of Branstree is singularly undistinguished, lying a short distance from the stile, and marked by a collapsed cairn of modest girth and a ground-level, circular triangulation station of a type rarely found in the Lake District.

From the summit, a clear grassy trod leads out to a couple of remarkable cairns on Artle Crag, to which you should press on. From the second cairn you easily reach a path beside the fence, and, by-passing an un-named summit off to the east and a survey pillar used during the construction of Haweswater, you simply follow the arrow-straight fenceline to the slight depression known as Captain Whelter Bog, a trap for the unwary only in very wet conditions. From here a clear path rises quickly onto the top of Selside Pike, marked by a large shelter-cairn.

On Selside Pike you quit the fenceline and launch into fell moorland without anything useful as a guide. But from the shelter two paths can be seen. Take the path on the left, slightly more pronounced, and good enough to guide you all the way down to intercept the Old Corpse Road west of Swindale Head **B**. The corpse road was used to convey the dead of Mardale on the backs of packhorses to the nearest churchyard for burial. The route crosses into Swindale and then traverses high moorland to Shap. The last such journey was made in 1736, by which time the right of burial had been granted to the tiny Holy Trinity church in Mardale Green, which recorded its

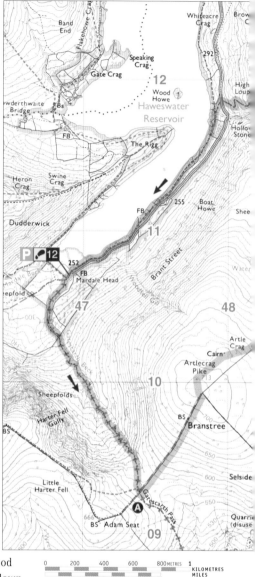

first burial in 1726. When, by 1936, plans to raise Haweswater and submerge Mardale Green were finalised, the burials made at Holy Trinity were disinterred and reburied at Shap.

You intercept the corpse road at a wooden pole; here, turn left, and walk gently uphill to the skyline. This is the high point of the crossing, a spot that must have brought a moment's

The summit of Branstree, with Selside Pike in the distance

The large cairn on Artle Crag

SCALE 1:25000 or 2½ INCHES to 1 MILE 4CM to 1KM

welcome respite to those in charge of conveying coffins across the moors, not least the packhorses.

The way is now all downhill, although there is nothing at all downhill about the quality of the landscape. For some distance the path potters about among numerous rocky outcrops and boggy dips, but then, with Haweswater and the fells to the west now fully in view, it begins its descent in earnest, dropping steeply to pass the ruins of a couple of buildings with the waterfalls of Rowantreethwaite Beck and Hopgill Beck appearing on the left.

The descending track eventually comes down to meet the valley road at a gate. Go left, crossing the road, to another gate opposite, from which a concessionary path runs back to Mardale Head at varying distances from the lakeshore. Its first task, however, is to cross the combined forces of Hopgill Beck and Rowantreethwaite Beck, which it does by means of a neat single-arch bridge. Beyond that, the path is clear enough and leads unerringly back to the start.

Hay Stacks

Start	Gatesgarth
Distance	4½ miles (7km)
Height gain	1,870 feet (570m)
Approximate time	3 hours
Parking	Pay and Display at Gatesgarth Farm
Route terrain	Good paths throughout; craggy fells, and a steep descent
Ordnance Survey maps	Landranger 90 (Penrith & Keswick), Explorer OL4 (The English Lakes – North-western area)

GPS waypoints

- NY 195 150
- Ⓐ NY 189 133
- Ⓑ NY 208 134

Tucked away in a corner of Buttermere, the summit of Hay Stacks is something of a puzzle. It enjoys no great elevation (1,958 feet or 597m), is surrounded by higher fells, and yet it holds great appeal for walkers. Perhaps it is because Hay Stacks is such a fine vantage point, or that it has dramatic cliffs overlooking Warnscale Bottom, or simply that the waters of Innominate Tarn hold the remains of Lakeland fell artist, Alfred Wainwright, and so draws legions of devotees.

Leave the parking area at Gatesgarth and find your way through gates onto a broad track that leads to Peggy's Bridge. Cross the bridge, and bear right briefly on a rising, rocky path (ignore the more level path heading north-west to Buttermere), before swinging to the left at a fence corner to begin a long and steady plod upwards. This used to be a packhorse route linking Buttermere with Ennerdale, and onward via Black Sail Pass into Mosedale and the head of Wasdale.

Charging upwards is only going to make you lathered and frazzled, but a relaxed gait will ease your way to the mountain pass linking Hay Stacks with High Crag, known as Scarth Gap Ⓐ. Here, turn left at a large cairn to begin a series of easy rocky ledges, where the use of hands will aid progress. Finally, just after passing a small tarn, you reach the summit, which takes the form of a short ridge with cairns at each end.

Perhaps surprisingly, the summit of Hay Stacks has quite a scattering of tarns, but the most dominant impression is that of High Crag, the high point of Buttermere Fell. It looks daunting from this angle, and its screes have been the downfall, literally, of unwary walkers. The view back across Buttermere to the fells at the head of Newlands is also fine; likewise the steep-sided form of Fleetwith Pike. Southwards, Great Gable and Kirk Fell manage to muscle in on the scene, blocking the end of unseen Ennerdale.

From the top of the fell you head along a clear and descending path that makes first for Innominate Tarn. Wainwright asked that his ashes be scattered here, and, in so doing, brought thousands of walkers to what was a

On the summit of Hay Stacks

splendidly peaceful and inspiring spot. There was even talk of renaming this nameless tarn, Wainwright Tarn, but thankfully common sense prevailed.

Beyond the tarn you encounter a lovely rocky passage leading to the outflow from the slender pool of

Blackbeck Tarn. Cross Black Beck, climbing for a short while before beginning a cross-country tramp, descending all the while to the slate spoil and buildings of Dubs Quarry, which was once served by a tramway from the top of Honister.

The ongoing path crosses Warnscale Beck and then bears left **B**, crossing the fell slope to meet a more pronounced track. Turn left onto this, and follow its course all the way down into Warnscale Bottom, descending through a mountain corrie that is both awesome and spectacular, daunting and inspirational. It is certainly rugged, craggy and wild.

Once securely at the foot of Warnscale, a path sweeps out easily to return to the road at Gatesgarth Farm. ●

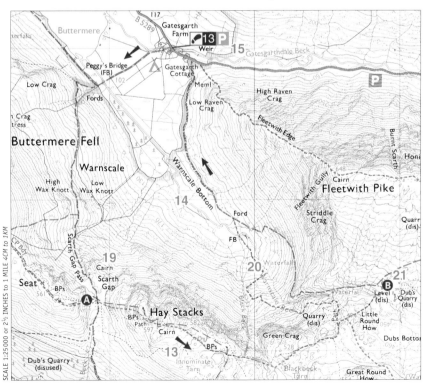

Sheffield Pike and Glenridding Dodd

Sheffield Pike and Glenridding Dodd

		GPS waypoints
Start	Glencoynedale foot	
Distance	5 miles (8km)	📷 NY 386 189
Height gain	1,935 feet (590m)	Ⓐ NY 375 184
Approximate time	3 hours	Ⓑ NY 362 182
Parking	NT car park (Pay and Display)	Ⓒ NY 373 178
Route terrain	Rough fell walking; steep descent; a little road walking	Ⓓ NY 378 175
Ordnance Survey maps	Landranger 90 (Penrith & Keswick), Explorer OL5 (The English Lakes – North-eastern area)	

Sheffield Pike suffers from the proximity of higher fare in the shape of Helvellyn, which tends to cloud the minds of the masses bound for the fells. But discerning fell explorers are always to be found pottering about on Sheffield Pike whether having ascended from Glenridding, or, as here, via lovely Glencoynedale. Adding Glenridding Dodd to the day's tally will tax no one, and reward with arguably the finest view there is of the southern end of Ullswater.

📷 A large car park just north of Glencoynedale is a near perfect place to begin. Turn right along the roadside footpath to reach the access track of Glencoyne Farm, here turning right.

On the way you cross Glencoyne Bridge, nice enough in itself, but especially significant to those who love the landscapes of the now defunct county of Westmorland, for Glencoyne Beck marks the boundary between the county and what was Cumberland.

As you approach Glencoyne Farm you cannot help but notice the distinctive, large, round chimneys that are so characteristic of the vernacular architecture of the 18th century, the farm being constructed in 1787. The farm was probably under the management of a yeoman farmer, one of that small, independent owner-occupier of farms that were a distinguishing feature of Cumbrian rural society. This secluded dwelling, is perhaps better seen across the pastures at the end of the walk, when it appears perfectly placed against the fells of Hart Side and Watermillock Common. John Robinson's *Guide to the Lakes* published in 1819, describes the farm '... embowered in trees, and standing under a range of rocks, which command a fine view of the middle bend of the lake.'

Take the only route available, going straight ahead through the garden of the cottage and soon begin climbing steeply, the way becoming a clear grooved track across a sloping pasture.

Continue with the path, now amply clear, to pass below the cottages at

Seldom Seen. The cottages, originally built for miners, now see service as holiday lets, and it is perhaps whimsical to imagine that the name refers to the out-of-the-way nature of this comely dale, which just gets better the higher you go.

The path presses on, as if going all the way into Glencoynedale, but at a low waymark, you bear left, ascending on a grassy path towards a wall and then running below it until you reach a gate **A** at a wall corner. Through the gate, turn right beside a wall, and follow this as it ascends steadily to a wall corner, with the great bowl of Glencoyne Head rising beyond to soft-moulded Green Side and Hart Side.

After a brief pull up from the gate, a splendid terrace path now follows for a while, until it starts to climb again as it crosses Bleabank Side and rises to a neat col at Nick Head **B**. Just as you approach Nick Head, the path divides. Branch left, taking the higher path with improving views across the intervening gulf of Glenridding to pyramidal Catstye Cam set against the dark cliffs of Helvellyn and the knobbly ridge of Striding Edge.

Just above Nick Head a metal boundary pole bears the date 1912 and the initials 'H' and 'M'; it marks the boundary of land between Howard of Greystoke and Marshall of Patterdale Hall; a similar pole will be found later on, near the top of Heron Pike. A peaty path now leads up to the top of Sheffield Pike, crowned by a fine cairn.

The continuation from Sheffield Pike summit needs a little care to begin with, just to ensure you locate the correct path, first to Heron Pike and then onwards and downwards. The main direction is south-east, and a clear and

0	200	400	600	800 METRES	1
					KILOMETRES
					MILES
0	200	400	600 YARDS	½	

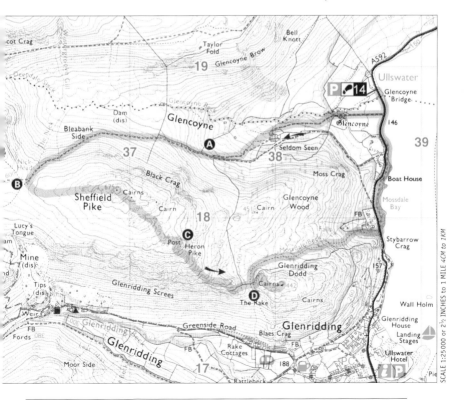

SCALE 1:25 000 or 2½ INCHES to 1 MILE 4CM to 1KM

Place Fell from Glenridding Dodd

continuous path takes you first to Heron Pike , from where you need to look to the southern side of the fell to locate another narrow path, tortuous and twisting in delightful fashion that guides you down to a wall gap just above the col linking to Glenridding Dodd .

The ascent of Glenridding Dodd is straightforward, setting off alongside a wall, but then abandoning the wall and curving back to the right to climb onto the top of the fell. The first large cairn you reach is the summit, but there are more cairns farther to the east, and the last of these marks a stupendous viewpoint that more than amply rewards the little extra effort.

Return to the col, and a gate through the wall, beyond which, a grassy trod sets off into Mossdale. The path soon joins Mossdale Beck, a delightful companion, with fine retrospective views of Heron Pike. Lower down, the path enters a spread of larch trees in a steep gully where a little ducking, diving and limbo dancing is needed to make progress. The path is continuous, but is not well used, and so it appears uncertain in places.

Eventually, the path descends to meet a fence. Turn left alongside this to a low step-stile nearby, over which you continue the descent to the valley road (A592); the last 100 yds of the descent are messy and slippery.

Cross the road and turn left, soon stepping off the road and onto a fine permissive path around the edge of Mossdale Bay that runs parallel with, but protected from, the busy road. It is a fine end to a fine walk, offering delightful cameos of the lake and its Norfolk Island through the trees. Where this path delivers you back on to the main road, cross over and follow the roadside footpath back to the car park. On the way, take a moment or two to look at Glencoyne Farm across the roadside pasture.

Beda Fell

		GPS waypoints
Start	Martindale	
Distance	5½ miles (9km)	 NY 433 190
Height gain	1,510 feet (460m)	Ⓐ NY 432 183
		Ⓑ NY 430 186
Approximate time	3 hours	Ⓒ NY 418 158
Parking	Martindale, limited at Howegrain Beck bridge	Ⓓ NY 433 165
Route terrain	Open fell ridge; numerous rocky outcrops; some road walking	
Ordnance Survey maps	Landranger 90 (Penrith & Keswick), Explorer OL5 (The English Lakes – North-eastern area)	

Separating the valleys of Boredale and Bannerdale at the bottom end of the long cul-de-sac that runs down the eastern shores of Ullswater from Pooley Bridge, Beda Fell will prove a most delightful surprise. This knobbly ridge offers an outstanding line of ascent that leads ultimately to the Angletarn Pikes, but crams a huge amount of walking pleasure into its circuit, leaving you with a distinct appetite for more.

The walk begins from the bridge spanning Howegrain Beck at Martindale, although there is more parking near the church on the hause to the north-east; this would add little to the overall distance, but means a short, sharp uphill finish.

Cross the bridge, following the road for around 150 yds to locate a broad track doubling back on the left. Turn up this, although you will find that it can be reached just as easily by a steep path from just after the bridge. Follow the track past a cottage, beyond which it continues parallel with a wall to rejoin the road at Winter Crag, a white-painted cottage Ⓐ. At the road, turn right at a slate waymark (signed 'Footpath to Boredale') onto a rising grassy path in a north-westerly direction.

For a while, the path and a wall climb together, but then part company as the wall descends to the right and the path climbs to a low col at the northern end of Beda Fell. A convenient bench Ⓑ, with a fine view over Boredale and Ullswater to Gowbarrow Fell, is an excellent place to regain your breath.

Now turn left to climb southwards

The summit of Beda Fell

along the ridge, the path rising repeatedly in simple steps as it tackles persistent rocky upthrusts. Higher up the ridge, the path divides, but it matters not which route you choose, as both rejoin later. That on the left is at an easier gradient, and is therefore a little longer.

Once the paths are reunited, the route continues along the crest of the ridge, now with the Beda Head, the summit of the ridge, in view.

The highest point of the fell is topped by two small cairns. Continue across the summit on a grassy path, and, after a few low grassy bumps, you begin a beautiful gradual descent towards Bedafell Knott, the final rock outcrop of the ridge before it links with Angletarn Pikes.

The top of Bedafell Knott is marked by a small cairn. Press on beyond it, but only for about 200 yds, until you reach a cross-path **C**, where there is also a cairn.

(Strong walkers may want to scamper further along the ridge to visit Angletarn Pikes, and then return to this crossing point, an ancient bridleway that would have seen considerable use

in years gone by as one of the principal thoroughfares across the valleys of Martindale Common.)

At the cross-path, turn abruptly left (north-east) on a stony path – and soon passing to the left of a ruin – to begin what will prove a delightful descent high above Bannerdale to the farm at Dale Head.

Across the valley, on the lower slopes of Wether Hill you can see a red-roofed building; this is The Bungalow, a hunting lodge built by the fifth Earl of Lonsdale, Hugh Cecil Lowther. The earl was a passionate sportsman and bon vivant, and known as 'England's greatest sporting gentleman'; he donated the original Lonsdale Belts for boxing.

Lord Lonsdale was also the inspiration for the Lonsdale cigar size, and was part of a famous wager with John Pierpoint Morgan over whether a man could circumnavigate the globe and remain unidentified.

He was known as the 'Yellow Earl' for his penchant for the colour. He was a founder and first president of the Automobile Association (AA) which adopted his livery.

The track comes down to a gate, from which it drops to run alongside a wall

Pikeawassa from Beda Fell

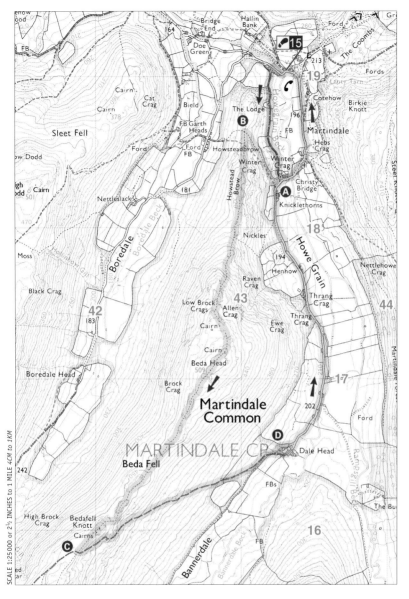

| 0 | 200 | 400 | 600 | 800 METRES | 1 KILOMETRES |
| 0 | 200 | 400 | 600 YARDS | ½ | MILES |

heading for Dale Head Farm **D** .

As you reach the farm there are two possible ways. One is to go through a gate on the right and walk through the farmyard; the other stays above the gate and follows a permissive route above the farm buildings and across a stream to locate a narrow gate. Both routes rejoin

at the road head, and now all that remains is to follow this quiet farm lane back to the white-painted building at Winter Crag **A**.

Here you have the choice of returning along the bridleway used at the start of the walk, or of remaining on the road to pass the nearby church and follow the road. At a road junction, you descend left to return to the bridge over Howegrain Beck and complete the walk. ●

Coniston Old Man

		GPS waypoints	
Start	Coniston		
Distance	5 miles (8km)		SD 304 975
Height gain	2,430 feet (740m)	**Ⓐ**	SD 285 981
Approximate time	3 hours	**Ⓑ**	SD 276 982
Parking	Coniston (Pay and Display)		
Route terrain	A rocky trail, on clear paths. *Parts can be confusing in mist, and the summit trig is very close to a steep drop*		
Ordnance Survey maps	Landranger 97 (Kendal & Morecambe), Explorer OL6 (The English Lakes – South-western area)		

The ascent begins along Church Beck before climbing through old quarries to reach Low Water and a final haul to the summit; it's a slaty way, and strewn with the remnant produce of man's industry. But when you reach the summit of the fell, there is a fine sensation of other-worldliness and achievement that reduces the spoil of toil to its rightful place in history, a brief passage of time. Nothing can detract from the wellbeing of conquering the Old Man.

From the main car park in Coniston, go left into the village and across the bridge, then immediately turning right along a minor road to the **Sun Hotel**. Here turn right onto a signposted path to the Old Man and Levers Water that pursues the course of Church Beck.

This pleasant start soon leads to a bridge at the entrance to Coppermines Valley. Keep left at this point, continuing on a less broad path and gaining height steadily as you rise to meet a well-constructed track at a bend **Ⓐ**, just to the north of The Bell. Turn right, following the track as it twists upwards through increasingly rough terrain and the spoil of quarrying generations past. Only a keen industrial archaeologist would find the untidy scenes of turmoil and dereliction attractive, yet the many

tumbled piles of slate, the rusted machinery and defunct buildings, arouse curiosity, about the men who toiled here, the hardships they faced, and the many dangers.

Some of the dangers are still present, especially if you venture near the main quarry, a vast hollow hacked from the hill, but unseen from the main path. At the top of a rise the path bends left then right. *If, before turning right, you continue ahead, you encounter a vast cavern, created by quarrymen. It is very dangerous now, having suffered roof collapses in the recent past. Do not enter, under any circumstances.*

Return to the main path, and ascend to reach Low Water 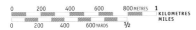 reposing in an enormous cirque of cliffs and steep, unstable slopes. This is one of Lakeland's grandest settings, the hue of the water, tinted blue by copper, injecting brightness into the scene.

The top of the Old Man lies directly above, but to reach it you must follow a rough and steep path zigzagging across the south wall of this corrie. Once at the top, turn right, and follow a broad, shaly path to the summit. The trig pillar is in a commanding position overlooking the Low Water basin.

The Old Man of Coniston was first ascended in 1792 by Captain Joseph Budworth, who had already that day walked from Ambleside to Coniston, to see the lake, and found himself unable to resist the challenge of the fell. Sustained only by brandy, he completed the first recorded ascent, and still walked back to Ambleside.

The top of the mountain used to possess three stone beacons – 'the Old Man', his 'Wife', and 'Son', clear evidence that others had ventured here ahead of Budworth. The largest of the three had a small chamber that provided rudimentary shelter. The disappearance of the beacons, it is alleged, was occasioned by Ordnance Survey engineers.

The measured distances and height gain for this walk assume a return by the outward route; a sufficient and satisfying prospect, without needing to extend the day any further. *Those with time, energy and inclination to do so, can effect a more circuitous return by continuing briefly northwards from the Old Man, before descending, left, on a rough path, to reach Goat's Hause, north-east of Goat's Water. From this broad boggy col, you can either descend to Goat's Water and follow a good path out to the Walna Scar Road, or ascend Dow Crag, to follow the long, undulating ridge to the Walna Scar Pass.* ●

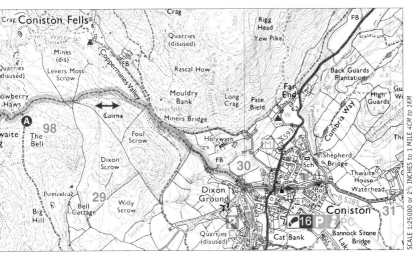

Wray Castle and Blelham Tarn

		GPS waypoints	
Start	Red Nab, High Wray	🖊	SD 385 995
Distance	6 miles (9.7km)	**A**	NY 376 013
Height gain	785 feet (240m)	**B**	NY 371 009
Approximate time	3 hours	**C**	NY 362 004
Parking	At start (use lane from High Wray)	**D**	SD 372 999
Route terrain	Lakeshore paths; farmland; woodland; some road walking	**E**	SD 375 989
		F	SD 378 986
Ordnance Survey maps	Landrangers 90 (Penrith & Keswick) and 97 (Kendal & Morecambe), Explorer OL7 (The English Lakes – South-eastern area)		

A chance to walk on the quiet side of Windermere, exploring a landscape that would have been familiar to Beatrix Potter, and which almost certainly sowed seeds in her imagination that later grew into her successful series of books. There is a great peace about this walk, which visits both Wray Castle, where Potter stayed as a child, and the beautifully set Blelham Tarn.

🖊 Begin from the parking area at Red Nab, at the shoreline end of the road from High Wray, and set off northwards along a broad lakeshore path and at the edge of broad-leaved Arthur Wood. In the woodland, sessile oak is the dominant tree species with an understorey of birch, holly and hazel, but there is also ash, wych elm and bird cherry. Great spotted woodpeckers favour these woodlands and it is a rare day when you do not see or at least hear them. There is also a good deal of evidence that the woodland was coppiced to produce charcoal for iron smelting and the manufacture of gunpowder. Tree bark was also used in the leather tanning process.

On leaving the woodland you arrive at High Wray Bay. Continue to a gate and through this carry on for another 45 yds to a second gate giving onto a permitted path into the grounds of Wray Castle. Return to the shore of the lake, and shortly climb left up a slope. At the top, bear right to a stile/gate to re-enter woodland, beyond which lies shapely Watbarrow Point sticking out into the lake like a knobbly thumb.

When the path intercepts another at a T-junction at Low Wray Bay **A**, turn left onto a gravel path that leads up towards Wray Castle.

Before doing so, a short diversion to the right is in order to visit the handsome Wray Castle Boathouse, which houses some of the fine ancient steamers that ply the lake. You can also make a short circuit of nearby Calf Parrock Coppice if time permits. You enter at a gate and can make an easy circular walk clockwise or anticlockwise.

Continue up the track, alongside a fence to just below the edifice of Wray Castle, and here turn right, still following a fenceline and on a path for the Gatehouse and Blelham Tarn. The path leads you up steps to the main entrance to the castle.

Wray Castle, then in the ancient county of Lancashire, was the creation of Dr James Dawson, a Liverpool surgeon who built the castle in 1840-7. There are towers, turrets, machicolations and battlements everywhere and a vast coach door (porte cochère), a feature of many 19th-century mansions. For that is what Wray Castle is, a mansion, built with the fortune of Dawson's wife, who alas did not like the building and refused to live in it. Beatrix Potter stayed at the castle when she was 16, and later bought much of the surrounding land, although she never owned the castle.

The castle, owned by the National Trust, is only very occasionally open to the public, although the grounds are freely accessible. They contain some outstanding tree specimens including Wellingtonia, redwood, weeping lime and Ginkgo biloba (also known as the Maidenhair Tree), a unique tree with no close-living relatives.

Continue out from the castle, along its surfaced driveway to reach the

High Wray Bay, Windermere

gatehouse, although it is possible to briefly divert into the ground of Wray church (also built by Dawson), where Hardwicke Rawnsley, co-founder of the National Trust, was vicar from 1877 until 1883.

At the road, turn right, descending gently. As the road starts to climb again, just after passing the turning to Low Wray campsite, go through a kissing-gate on the left **B** and along a permitted path beside the road. After 200 yds you arrive at a road gate on your right. Here, turn left onto a bridleway that passes to the south of a hummock known as Randy Pike. When the track forks, bear left across a hummocky pasture on a broad grassy path that leads to a gate giving into sparse broad-leaved woodland. The track leads to a shallow ford, crossed on stepping stones, just after which you keep to the left of a wall to enter the next pasture. The path stays by the wall to reach another permitted footpath at a signpost **C**.

Turn left for High Tock How, following a path around the south-western end of Blelham Tarn that soon runs alongside a fence. The path crosses a neat stone bridge after which it rises as a broad track to a stone barn. Just past the barn, cross a step-stile onto a path for High Tock How. Walk up to another gate and beyond this descend around the edge of rough pasture to the access to the farm. Turn right to walk out to a lane. Turn right again, climbing briefly to a higher road.

Turn left, and now follow the road, taking care against approaching traffic, for ½ mile, passing an interesting stone-built well 'In Memory of Happy Days', built in 1891.

The roadside hedge has been used for the traditional boundary building technique of hedge laying, a country skill found throughout Britain and Ireland.

As you reach High Wray Farm, leave the road by branching right onto a roughly surfaced track **D** signposted for Basecamp and Claife Heights. Continue past the turning into Basecamp, now following a broad woodland trail. Ignore diverging footpaths and stay on the main trail, climbing steadily for some distance into an area that has been cleared. Gradually the trail starts to descend, and when the track forks **E** bear left, taking the lower of two trails.

At a multiple track junction **F**, turn left onto a bridleway for Belle Grange. The track, which is quite rough underfoot, descends through splendid, mature mixed woodland. At the next path junction, continue descending towards the lakeshore.

The track eventually comes down to reach the boundary wall of Belle Grange, which is followed out to intercept the lakeshore path. Turn left for High Wray, and follow the track back to the Red Nab car park. ●

Blencathra: Hall's Fell Ridge and Doddick Fell

		GPS waypoints
Start	Threlkeld	
Distance	3¾ miles (6km)	📍 NY 324 255
Height gain	2,395 feet (730m)	Ⓐ NY 324 261
		Ⓑ NY 323 277
Approximate time	3 hours	Ⓒ NY 329 277
Parking	Limited roadside parking in village; car park at NY 318 256	
Route terrain	Rough fell walking, craggy outcrops, scree; *difficult in winter conditions*	
Ordnance Survey maps	Landranger 90 (Penrith & Keswick), Explorer OL5 (The English Lakes – North-eastern area)	

There is a widely sustained view among enthusiasts of Lakeland fell walking that to ascend Blencathra by Hall's Fell Ridge is one of the finest, if not the finest, route to the summit of any of the Lake District fells. Combining this ascent with a descent of adjacent Doddick Fell, another splendid route, proves to be a most exhilarating excursion, one that in winter conditions calls in places for all the skills one might expect of an Alpine climber. This is NOT a walk for beginners; it is energetic from the off and requires an element of scrambling on Hall's Fell Ridge.

📍 The ascent starts in the village of Threlkeld, famed for its huntsmen, many of whom are named and remembered on a monument in the churchyard. Of interest, too, is the **Horse and Farrier Inn**, one of the oldest in the Lake District, and sometime refreshment stop for Wordsworth as he travelled between Grasmere and Penrith on postmasterly duties, often accompanied by de Quincey.

The village is now bypassed by the busy A66, but soon after leaving the A-road, turn right onto a minor back road (Fell Side) that leads to a bridleway on the left leading up to Gategill Farm Ⓐ. On reaching the farm, pass through a gate into the farmyard, passing between

buildings to a double gate that gives onto an enclosed pathway above the narrow ravine and cascades of Gate Gill.

As you walk on, suddenly a stunning view appears of Hall's Fell Top rising above the as yet unseen recesses of Gate Gill. The path leads to another gate and beyond bears right, across Gate Gill, in the vicinity of the disused Woodend Lead Mine.

Once across the stream, grind steadily up a steeply ascending path, that threads bracken, heather and low rock outcrops to gain a foothold on the broad base of Hall's Fell ridge. The route is never in doubt, and frequent rest halts allow you to take in the fecund richness of the valley fields below, the ever-widening panorama of Great and Little Mell Fells, and the blue-green fells around Derwentwater.

After what seems like a long haul, the gradient eases, and the ridge begins to narrow, at first only marginally, and then more dramatically, as Doddick Fell and the more bulkier Scales Fell come into view. A wide outcrop of rock spanning the width of the ridge marks the start of the section known as Narrow Edge, a succession of shapely outcrops, mini-towers, gullies and ledges that walkers adept at scrambling will find delightful to tackle head on. Less confident walkers will find a way round for much of the ascent on one side or other of the ridge, though in the end it becomes easier to deal with the ridge than to try avoiding it.

The great beauty of the ridge is that it leads unerringly to the summit **B**. The view, not surprisingly, is outstanding, and reaches far into the heart of Lakeland as well as northwards and north-west to the lower Northern Fells and Skiddaw.

Doddick Fell ridge

The continuation to Doddick Fell bears right (initially north-east) following a broad path and the escarpment above Doddick Gill. When, at a cairn, this path forks, go right, and continue descending, an attractive array of rock turrets delineating the right-hand edge. To the left, Sharp Edge eases into view above unseen Scales Tarn, while beyond this gap rise the mounds of Bannerdale Crags and Bowscale Fell.

The descending path continues to Scales Fell, probably the easiest way down, but en route it becomes possible to move right on a narrow trod leading to the crags at the top of Doddick Fell **C**. The start of the way down Doddick Fell takes to a narrow shaly path flirting with rock outcrops, *maintaining a*

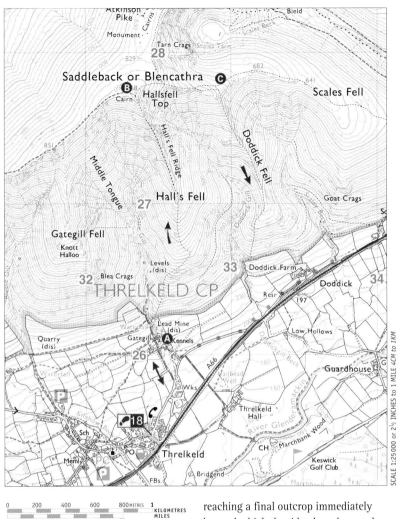

SCALE 1:25000 or 2½ INCHES to 1 MILE 4CM to 1KM

```
0      200    400    600    800 METRES   1
                                    KILOMETRES
                                    MILES
0      200    400    600 YARDS    ½
```

steepness *that calls for caution for some way down the ridge.* The whole of this upper section may be avoided by staying on the Scales Fell path for a little longer, to reach a cairn that marks the upper limit of a more regular path sliding across the fellside to meet the main Doddick ridge beneath the most awkward section.

The continuation down the ridge is a pleasure to walk. It gives fine views of Clough Head and Great Dodd, and Hall's Fell Top in particular, as it passes through a mantle of heather before reaching a final outcrop immediately beyond which the ridge broadens and plummets to the buildings and green pastures of Doddick Farm.

The route now moves right, descending gradually to reach the intake wall not far east of Doddick Gill. Follow the path, right, alongside the wall and when it starts to move away, towards the gill, stay with the wall to its end, there turning left to drop down to cross the gill at a ford. A good path leads on then above the ongoing intake wall, and pleasantly across the base of Hall's Fell ridge back to Gate Gill near the Woodend mine, from where you simply retrace your outward steps.   ●

Rough Crag and High Street

		GPS waypoints
Start	Mardale Head	
Distance	5½ miles (9km)	NY 469 107
Height gain	2,100 feet (640m)	**A** NY 473 114
Approximate time	3½ hours	**B** NY 442 113
Parking	Mardale Head	**C** NY 452 096
Route terrain	Rough mountain walking; long ascents and descents, steep in places	
Ordnance Survey maps	Landranger 90 (Penrith & Keswick), Explorer OL5 (The English Lakes – North-eastern area)	

During the course of a year, many walkers visit the flat-topped summit of High Street; it has the attraction of elevation, good views and fits neatly into a number of entertaining circuits. But only discerning walkers take to the rocky approach offered by Rough Crag. Close scrutiny of the map reveals a more sensible line to the south, one that becomes an outstanding ridge walk.

The walk begins from the car park at the road end in Mardale. Parking is limited and free, so arrive early. The setting is magnificent, with high, rocky, steep-sided fells forming the valley head. Go through the gate at the end of the car park, and turn right beside a wall, to cross Mardale Beck, and right again, heading for the mature stand of larch and spruce that colonise The Rigg. As you approach the trees, the path starts rising, and finally meets the low end of a ridge at a gap in a wall **A**.

Just after the wall, go left, over a small hillock cloaked in bracken, with the formidable end of Rough Crag towering above you. It seems impregnable, but a path threads a way through or round all obstacles on the way. The going is far less rough than the name suggests, but it remains steep, at least until the summit, marked by a large cairn, is reached.

The view from the ridge never fails to impress: to the south lies a deep bowl containing Blea Water, overlooked by the slopes of High Street; to the north, Kidsty Pike rises above the wide cove of Riggindale. Golden eagles are often seen above Riggindale and the surrounding fells, though their eyrie is zealously guarded by members of the RSPB. *You can ease their vigil by keeping strictly to the path over Rough Crag during the breeding season (from mid-March to September).*

Continue along

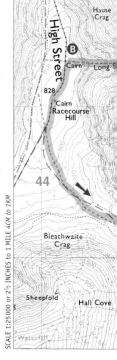

the ridge and descend a little to a grassy col, Caspel Gate, where there is a small pool. Beyond this you engage an airy, twisting path ascending Long Stile, finally to reach the northern end of High Street **B**. The summit lies a couple of minutes south, and the simplest way of finding it in mist is to walk ahead (west) from the top of Long Stile until you intersect a dilapidated wall, and then follow this left (south) to the trig pillar.

From the summit, walk beside the wall to intercept a stony path that crosses a grassy link to Mardale Ill Bell: the right of way shown on the map across High Street does not exist on the ground. But, on a clear day, you can more or less head straight for Mardale Ill Bell. This last of the Kentmere west side fells forms a thumb of land separating Kentdale and Mardale, and by moving north for a short distance

from the main path as you reach the cairned summit, you discover a stunning view of Blea Water lying in its corrie below.

Continue with the path across Mardale Ill Bell, and follow its descent, occasionally via stone steps, to Nan Bield Pass **C**, an ancient packhorse route crossing point. 'Nan' derives from the Welsh, and means a brook or a gorge, while 'bield' means a sheltered place. A small shelter sits in the middle of the narrow col.

Turn northwards (left) from Nan Bield and begin a stony descent, the path casting about through rocky terrain, eventually to reach a cluster of low stone shelters beside Small Water. Stepping stones usually help you cross Small Water Beck providing delightful cascades as you follow its course towards Haweswater. But steadily the path moves away from the beck as it rounds the northern end of Harter Fell and finally descends to Mardale Head.●

0	200	400	600	800 METRES	1
					KILOMETRES
					MILES
0	200	400	600 YARDS	½	

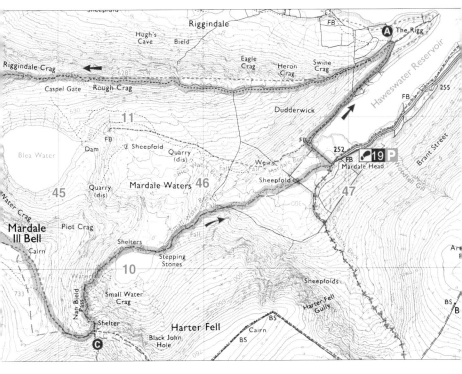

Bannerdale Crags and Souther Fell

		GPS waypoints	
Start	Mungrisdale		
Distance	6¾ miles (10.8km)	✏	NY 364 302
Height gain	2,015 feet (614m)	Ⓐ	NY 356 302
		Ⓑ	NY 327 292
Approximate time	3½ hours	Ⓒ	NY 343 279
Parking	Roadside parking area (honesty payment) opposite the Recreation Rooms	Ⓓ	NY 354 291
Route terrain	Stony tracks, fell and moorland paths		
Ordnance Survey maps	Landranger 90 (Penrith & Keswick), Explorer OL5 (The English Lakes – North-eastern area)		

Bannerdale Crags are never going to be seen criss-crossed with rock climbing paraphernalia, they are too friable and shaly for that, but they do have quite a shapely profile and a dramatic little ascent if you follow this walk. Elsewhere the route visits the source of the River Glenderamackin and a grassy fell once inhabited by a spectral army.

✏ Set off by crossing the footbridge over the Glenderamackin and walk up to the **Mill Inn**; pass behind the inn and walk out to rejoin the main valley road. Take the first turning on the left, past the telephone box, following a broad stony track. Continue to the narrow wooden footbridge Ⓐ spanning Bullfell Beck, and a short way farther on you have a choice of routes. *Either stay with the main track and ascend easily to the rim of Bannerdale, and there turn left to walk around to the top of Bannerdale Crags. Or (the measured route and a little more challenging) abandon the main rising track by branching left onto a narrower path that stays in the company of the River Glenderamackin.*

Continue following the riverside path until you reach Bannerdale Beck, issuing from the valley on your right.

You need to cross the beck, and then immediately leave the main path and take to the steep slope on your right by a narrower zigzagging path. This, for want of a name no one seems to have given it, is Bannerdale Rigg, and it is quite delightful. That initial steepness is short-lived and then the ridge continues to a small topknot before pressing on to the foot of a cascade of mining spoil hard pressed against the crags of Bannerdale.

Go forward with the ridge path into the mining spoil. Improbable as it seems a path does thread a way through this hiatus to reach a grassy shoulder just below the summit of Bannerdale Crags. The path is narrow, and casts about all the time, but it is clear and easy enough to follow. Once on the shoulder above, move right to a large cairn that is the

Looking across from Souther Fell to Bannerdale Crags

popular top of the fell, with a lovely view east across Souther Fell to the distant Pennines and Cross Fell.

The cairn is not the highest point of the fell; this lies a short distance to the west, and a broad grassy trod leads you that way. The true summit is marked by a rather dismal, flattened cairn, but the whole scene here is dominated by the huge bulk of Blencathra, which from this angle shows why it has the alternative name of 'Saddleback'.

From the cairn, continue roughly westwards following a now descending quad bike track. Follow the path to its lowest point on a col **B** overlooking Mungrisdale Common. Here, turn left (south-east), taking the lower of two paths that leads down to the headwaters of the River Glenderamackin. A short way down the path you meet a spring that is the primary source of the river, one that journeys only as far as Threlkeld, where it becomes the River Greta.

The path down the valley is a delight to follow, hemmed in on both sides by steep-sided grassy fell slopes, which, to

the west, lead up into the hollow containing Scales Tarn above which rises the narrow rocky crest of Sharp Edge, one of the slimmest and airiest mountain ridges in Lakeland.

Eventually, as you follow the descending path, you reach a point where a narrow path branches right, down to a footbridge **C** spanning the river. Go this way, cross the bridge, and climb the path beyond.

The path leads to a broad grassy col beyond which lies Mousthwaite Comb, but you do not go quite that far. Once on the col, almost immediately you encounter a cross-path. Here, turn left, and climb steadily onto the grassy slopes of Souther Fell.

Souther Fell has quite a place in Lakeland history. Harriet Martineau (1802–76), the English writer who eventually made her home in Ambleside, describes in *A Complete Guide to the English Lakes* how, 'This Souther, or Soutra Fell, is the mountain on which ghosts appeared in myriads, at intervals during ten years of the last century – presenting precisely the same appearance to 26 chosen witnesses, and to all the inhabitants of all the cottages within view of the mountain; and for a space of two hours and a half at one time – the spectral show being then closed by darkness.'

The story starts on Midsummer Eve in 1735, when a farm servant saw the whole of the eastern side of the mountain covered with marching troops coming from the northern end and disappearing on the summit. Predictably, when he told his story 'he was insulted on all hands'. Two years later, also on Midsummer Eve, the farmer himself saw men on the summit, apparently following their horses, but when he looked again a few minutes later, they were mounted and followed by 'an interminable array of troops, five abreast, marching from the eminence [at the northern end] and over the cleft'. Now it was the farmer's turn to be insulted. So, on Midsummer Eve of 1745, the year of the Jacobite rebellion, the famer expressly invited 26 people to witness the occurrence. This time

carriages were interspersed with the troops; and everybody knew that no carriages ever had been, or could be, on the summit of Souther Fell. 'The multitude was beyond imagination; for the troops filled a space of half-a-mile, and marched quickly until night hid them, – still marching. There was nothing vaporous or indistinct about the appearance of these spectres. So real did they seem that some of the people went up, the next morning, to look for the hoof-marks of the horses; and awful it was to them to find not one foot-print on heather or grass.' Everything the witnesses saw was attested by them before a magistrate, when it also came out that two other people had seen the same thing in 1743.

Make of that what you will. But

On Souther Fell

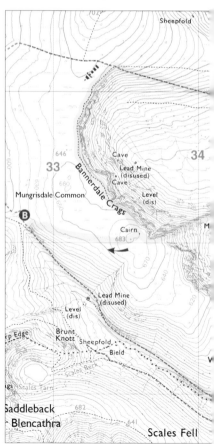

maybe as you walk across the broad grassy ridge that is Souther Fell, you may occasionally feel a chill of something past breathing down your neck.

When the ongoing path forks, you can take either route; the one on the right keeping to the high ground, the one on the left heading for a large cairn from which there is a fine view of your line of ascent along Bannerdale Rigg, and north to Bowscale Fell. A path leads from the cairn back to the high ground.

Except to the extent that GPS readings give a different height 1,758 feet (536m) to the map 1,710 feet (522m), the summit of the fell **D** is an anticlimax, a small shaly outcrop with no other distinguishing feature. Keep on following the high ground, a clear path leading you to the end of the fell, where the path drops in stages to one final steep flourish. Stay with it and aim for a fence through heather, and here turn right following a narrow path that leads down to meet a wall. Turn right beside the wall, and then, later, at a fence corner you can turn left and descend to meet a lane at a gate. Through the gate follow the lane down until you can branch right on a walled track towards a ford across the Glenderamackin. Just before the ford, cross a stone stile on the right and the footbridge beyond. Over the bridge, turn left to a gap stile in a wall, and after this walk up to the road near High Beckside. Turn left to return to Mungrisdale and complete the walk. ●

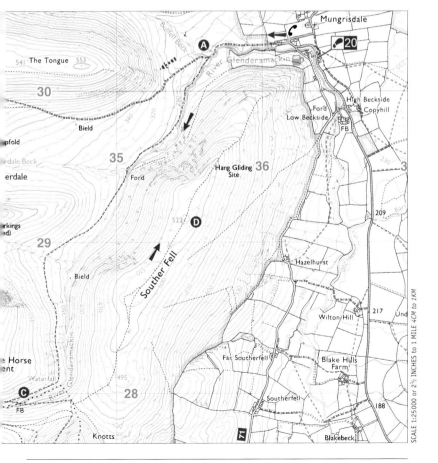

SCALE 1:25000 or 2½ INCHES to 1 MILE 4CM to 1KM

Wetherlam

		GPS waypoints	
Start	High Tilberthwaite	🥾	NY 306 010
Distance	5½ miles (8.8km)	Ⓐ	NY 304 007
Height gain	2,295 feet (700m)	Ⓑ	NY 293 016
Approximate time	3½ hours	Ⓒ	NY 287 011
Parking	At start	Ⓓ	SD 293 990
Route terrain	Rough fell slopes; *steep ascent and descent; the top of Wetherlam is confusing in mist*		
Ordnance Survey maps	Landrangers 90 (Penrith & Keswick) and 96 (Barrow-in-Furness & South Lakeland), Explorer OL6 (The English Lakes – South-western area)		

A popular tourist place during Victorian times, Tilberthwaite Gill is a natural gorge of considerable beauty, through which flows Yewdale Beck, though the stream is generally known as Tilberthwaite Gill. The region also saw its share of slate quarrying during the 19th century. Overlording the gill, and a landscape that has notable appeal, rises Wetherlam, a fine, rugged, satisfying summit, here ascended from Tilberthwaite by a justifiably popular route.

The hamlet of Low Tilberthwaite lies secreted within enfolding fells, along a minor road that runs acutely away from the A593 about 1½ miles north of

Low Tilberthwaite

Coniston. Take care as you drive along this winding road – the scenery is a great distraction.

🥾 From the lower edge of a commodious (but in summer inadequate) car park a flight of slate steps ascends quickly through quarry spoil to a path junction. *On the way you pass Penny Rigg Quarry, which is worth a peek, but keep children and dogs under control since there are sudden and unfenced drops within the quarry.*

At the path junction Ⓐ you have a choice of ways. Either (a) go right, and descend to a bridge spanning Tilberthwaite Gill, and then steeply (on an unstable footpath) to join a former miners' track. Turn left. Or, (b) climb left for a little pleasant cavorting with rocky knuckles *(slippery when wet)*, before the path opens out and swings round to head towards Crook Beck.

More evidence of quarrying now appears, in a vast mountain arena that is a fascinating place for the curious; but a dangerous one, too.

Slate quarrying has been a lasting source of wealth for the Lakeland economy, though inland quarries, like those above Tilberthwaite, had a limited period of prosperity, often supplying only a local market. Yet, as long ago as 1818, merchants, like Thomas Rigge of Hawkshead, were exporting Tilberthwaite green slate, carrying it via Coniston Water to Greenodd, from where it went by sloop to seaports throughout England and Ireland.

Pass through the quarrying area, *but do keep well away from shafts and adits.* By a footbridge, cross Tilberthwaite Gill, and climb to the miners' track joined earlier by walkers who chose to cross the gill lower down. Turn left along the track to begin a splendid, rising walk that visits the ruins of Hellen's Mine, and skirts the marshlands of Dry Cove, once flooded to provide power for a water wheel at the Tilberthwaite Mine, to arrive at the Borlase Mine, high above the cove.

Take a rough but enjoyable path,

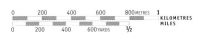

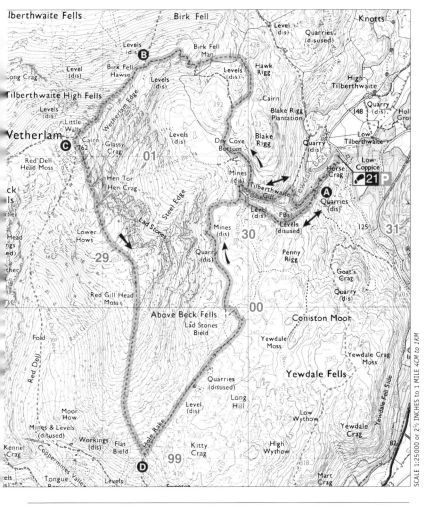

Coniston Water from Wetherlam

ascending right, in zigzags to reach Birk Fell Hawse **B**, a narrow neck of land linking Wetherlam and nearby Birk Fell. This upper section of the walk, with its retrospective view of Dry Cove and the quarrylands beyond, is splendid; the arrival at Birk Fell Hawse, even better. For here, the ground falls, almost unnoticed, across Greenburn, before sprawling onwards across the fells above Langdale and out to the distant Scafells.

The ascent to the top of Wetherlam now pursues a fine, rocky (and, if you want it, scrambly) ridge, networked by paths, all of which guide you ever upwards. The top of the fell **C** is a vast rocky platform, with views as far-reaching as Ingleborough in Craven. Much nearer lies the Old Man of Coniston and Swirl How, separated by the modest hump of Brim Fell. Among the summit rocks there are many nooks in which to shelter, or you could press on towards a conspicuous cairn to the south (signalling the eventual way off), and then deviate to the right for a secluded break gazing across at the Old Man.

The cairn lies along a steadily improving path that descends for quite some distance through rocky knolls and tarn-filled hollows – a delightful experience – eventually to move left (south-east) to fall gradually to a path near the top of Hole Rake Pass **D**. Go left, along the path, passing a small reed-filled tarn, and continue, north-east and north, in the company of Crook Beck, until you ultimately return to the quarry site at the head of Tilberthwaite Gill.

You can return to the car park quickly by turning right, along the path on the south side of the gill, or, preferably, re-cross the footbridge ahead (used earlier in the walk), and turn right to reach the miners' track. Go right again, now descending the track, with Tilberthwaite Gill below on the right, and continue a pleasurable descent to a gate/wall just above Low Tilberthwaite.

Continue with the path, down and round to the cottages below, where you will find a fine example of a cottage with a spinning gallery, from which wool would be hung to dry.

On reaching the road, the car park remains only a few strides away to the right.

Torver Commons and Walna Scar

		GPS waypoints
Start	Coniston	SD 304 975
Distance	8¼ miles (13.2km)	**A** SD 300 947
Height gain	1,425 feet (435m)	**B** SD 285 945
Approximate time	4 hours	**C** SD 273 965
Parking	Coniston (Pay and Display)	**D** SD 289 970
Route terrain	Lakeshore paths; woodland; rugged moors and mosses; stony fell tracks	**E** SD 285 981
Ordnance Survey maps	Landranger 97 (Kendal & Morecambe), Explorer OL7 (The English Lakes – South-eastern area)	

The Torver Commons cover a wide area. The lakeside commons offer relaxed strolling before a complete contrast by climbing up to an ancient packhorse thoroughfare, the Walna Scar Road, that runs along the rugged base of the Coniston Fells. The walk concludes with a loop northwards to gaze down into Coppermines Valley.

Leave the centre of Coniston along the A593, and as you approach the edge of the village centre, turn left into Lake Road. As you reach the Lake Road Estate, where the road bends to the left, leave it by climbing over a stile on the right into a large pasture and onto a footpath for Torver via the Lakeshore. The path is level and offers fine views of the Coniston Fells, and glimpses of Coniston Water through lakeside trees. Pass through a gate and continue beside a fence towards a small wooded mound. When the fence ends, turn left following a wide track down towards the lakeshore.

As you approach the lakeshore the path bends towards a farm and camping site based around Coniston Hall. Pass to the right of Coniston Hall, and stay on a surfaced lane to pass an outbuilding and then continue on a clear lane. After passing through a gate you enter the grounds of a seasonal campsite. Follow the main surfaced track, drawing ever closer to the lake, and then at a waymark branching left onto a stony track that leads to a gate in a wall, beyond which you now follow the lakeshore.

Five miles long, and with a depth approaching 200 feet, Coniston Water is the third largest of the lakes. In 1967, Donald Campbell was killed on Coniston Water while attempting the water speed record, which he had originally broken in 1955. After a couple of gates you reach a signpost pointing a way to the right for Torver; ignore this, and keep on along the lakeshore towards Torver Common Wood. Shortly the path is deflected a little way inland to pass round a small copse, but soon enters Torver Commons, where you return to the lakeshore.

When you next reach a signpost for

Torver **A**, turn right, leaving the lakeshore. The path climbs to leave the Torver Commons at a gate, beyond which it continues through more light woodland, with Dow Crag and the Old Man of Coniston once more in view. After passing through a couple of gates and some derelict buildings, the path becomes enclosed between a hedgebank and a moss-covered wall.

You pass Brackenbarrow Farm, and then walk out along a broader access track to intercept a narrow lane. Cross this and go over a step-stile opposite and then take to a muddy path across rough pasture to a kissing-gate, beyond which the path is less of a quagmire. After a short section of boardwalk, keep to the right-hand edge of a field to reach the A593.

Turn left and walk beside the road for about 100 yds, and then leave the main road at a bend **B**, by turning right up a narrow lane to Scarr Head. Follow the lane, signposted for Tranearth and Walna Scar, turning right at Scarr Head Cottage onto a surfaced bridleway. When the surfacing ends a rough track takes over.

Eventually, at a barn, the track breaks free of constraining walls, and continues across rough moorland with outstanding views of the Coniston Fells. A concrete

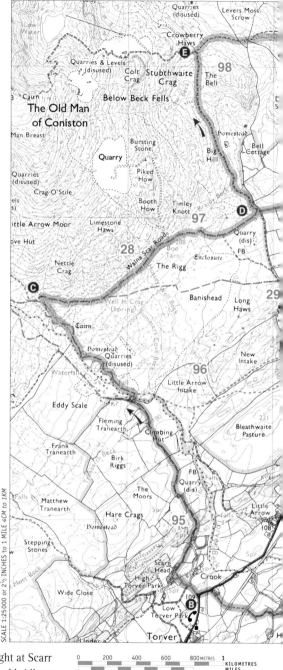

SCALE 1:25 000 or 2½ INCHES to 1 MILE 4CM to 1KM

footbridge takes you over Tranearth Beck, beyond which the track continues towards an area of quarry spoil.

After three gates in quick succession, you cross Torver Beck. Stay with the

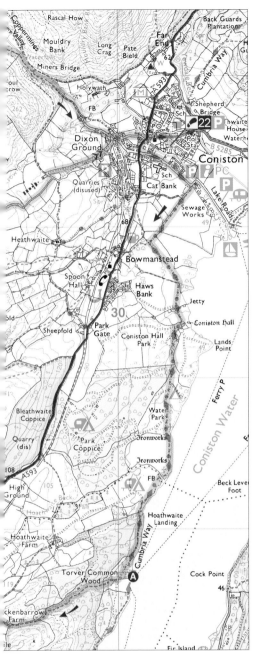

little importance, which is used. The road is a clear stony track running roughly east to west, and, if you stay approximately along the line of Torver Beck or any of the streams flowing down from Little Arrow Moor, you will intercept it. When you do, turn right, and follow it through twists and turns and narrow rock passages, and passing reed-filled Boo Tarn, until it ends at a gate beyond which lies a surfaced lane. Here you have the choice of taking the lane, which will provide you with a direct return to Coniston village.

But the walk continues by turning left **D** along what is the most popular route onto the Old Man of Coniston. The track climbs steadily, passing the very shapely minor top called The Bell – you can make an easy diversion to include this superb vantage point if time permits, using a clear grassy path that branches right from the main stony track you are following.

Eventually, just after passing through a couple of rocky jaws, as the Old Man path circles to the left **E**, you can leave it for a clear path descending on the right towards Coniston, and offering a fine view, as does The Bell, of Coppermines Valley.

track as it now bears to the left below slate spoil. Once above this, the track bears to the right to pass around the quarry itself, into which a fine waterfall plummets, filling a lake with no apparent outflow.

A number of tracks now lead up to the Walna Scar Road **C**, and it is of

The path is straightforward and leads all the way down to the outskirts of Coniston. At Dixon Ground Farm, you reach a lanehead. Keep forward, and at the **Sun Hotel** turn left and walk down to the village centre, opposite the **Yewdale Inn**, from where you retrace your steps to the car park. ●

Rosthwaite and Stonethwaite

		GPS waypoints	
Start	Rosthwaite	🥾	NY 258 148
Distance	9 miles (14.5km)	**Ⓐ**	NY 251 151
Height gain	850 feet (260m)	**Ⓑ**	NY 250 139
Approximate time	4 hours	**Ⓒ**	NY 235 121
Parking	Rosthwaite National Trust car park	**Ⓓ**	NY 252 137
Route terrain	Generally level; stony paths; some minor road walking	**Ⓔ**	NY 272 126
Ordnance Survey maps	Landranger 90 (Penrith & Keswick), Explorer OL4 (The English Lakes – North-western area)		

This delightful walk is filled with geological significance, and spends most of its time in an area that once held two or even three post-glacial lakes, long since disappeared. Anyone planning post-graduate research in glacial geology would have many field days here. The walk begins from the small National Trust car park at Rosthwaite, but, if this is full, begin at Seatoller instead, or Stonethwaite.

🥾 Leave the car park, and turn right along the narrow lane into Rosthwaite village, and then bear right to follow a walled, stony track. As the track bends right on meeting the River Derwent it is sometimes possible to cross the river on stepping stones, in which case do so, or stay with the track to New Bridge, just before which there is an attractive pollarded ash tree.

Cross New Bridge Ⓐ and turn left to a footbridge, followed by another, after which you take to a narrow path parallel with the river and alongside a fence. At a gate you reach those stepping stones again, and now continue beside a wall initially crossing many tree roots that can be slippery when wet. Stay along the true left bank of the river, and press on to a kissing-gate from which you go forward past a

Stonethwaite Valley

Langstrath Beck

cottage onto a track to reach a surfaced lane. Here, turn right towards Borrowdale Youth Hostel.

Pass in front of the hostel, and then keep forward, still beside the river, following a broad track. Stay ahead through an awkward rocky section, just where the river changes direction.

On the opposite bank you will notice a small slope where the under-soil is filled with all sizes of boulders. This is actually glacial moraine, a line of debris that continues across the valley at this point, and which forced the river to alter its course.

A short section of glaciated rock has chains attached for security, not exactly Via Ferrata, but welcome enough if the rocks are wet. Just after this, descend briefly to the left and then almost immediately go right, over a rocky shoulder to gain a fence-side path leading to a gate.

If you look into the field on the left, you will notice what geologists call a 'break of slope' along the field edge; this is quite marked, and shows the edge of either a small glacial lake held back by that moraine, or the banks of the river along an earlier course. No one knows which for sure; it's up for research.

Now continue beside the wall, below beech and oak woodland to reach another kissing-gate from which the stony path continues across a brackeny slope. When the path forks **B**, keep right. *By branching left you go down to Folly Bridge and can then follow a field edge path out to meet the valley road at Strands Bridge. This is a shortcut, should you choose not to take the Seathwaite section of the walk. You rejoin the main route at the road, and there turn left.*

The right branch takes you on to reach the car park at Seatoller, and out to the Honister road. Turn left down the road, and shortly bear right along the lane to Seathwaite. It's about a mile of a walk down to Seathwaite, and generally untroubled, but this is one of the main access routes for those wanting to climb Scafell Pike, so take care against approaching traffic. The **café at Seathwaite Farm** offers a welcome break (and there are **toilets** here).

Just past the café, after the last of the buildings, you can turn left onto a footpath **C** – part of the Allerdale Ramble – that takes you back on the opposite side of the valley, below Thornythwaite Fell and past Thornythwaite Farm, to rejoin the valley road at Strands Bridge. On reaching the valley road, turn right, and cross the road to the footpath opposite.

After about 175 yds, leave the road by branching right onto a public footpath **D** (the Tarn at Leaves path), but soon leave this by striking left across Combe Gill for Stonethwaite – the path is not quite as shown on maps, nor is it a right of way, but its use is permitted. Follow it until it turns left into a wall corner, and here pass through a gate in a wall corner, and go right through a gate gap, and then forward along a farm track, following this to reach a cluster of cottages near St Andrew's Church on the edge of Stonethwaite.

Go through a gate and turn right to pass the church. Follow the road out to a junction just past a row of garages. Turn right again and follow the road into Stonethwaite village. *As you reach a red telephone box, you can shorten the walk by turning left down a path to Stonethwaite Bridge, after which you turn left, having rejoined the full route.*

Walk into the village, passing the welcome **Peathouse Tea and Coffee**

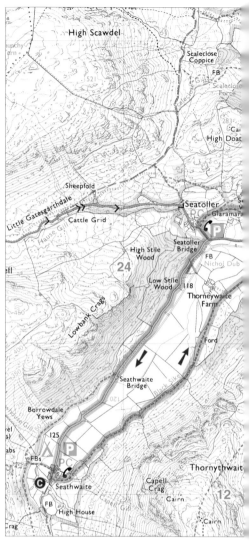

shop, and then the **Langstrath Country Inn**. Just past the inn, bear right onto a rising lane (ignore the footpath through a gate on the left), which soon becomes a stony track.

Continue following the track, which follows a delightful course above a camp site and keeps on around the foot of Bessyboot, with the great profile of Eagle Crag ahead. Finally, the track breaks out into rough pasture. Here, bear right alongside a wall, following a stony track that soon bears right into Langstrath. Go through a gate and

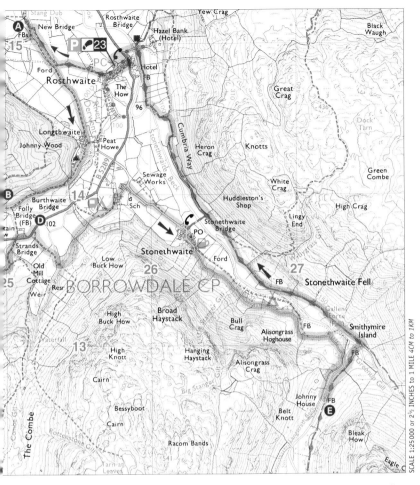

SCALE 1:25000 or 2½ INCHES to 1 MILE 4CM to 1KM

keep on along the Langstrath track to reach a footbridge spanning Langstrath Beck **E**.

On the other side, turn left and follow a path that leads to another footbridge spanning Greenup Gill.

Beyond Greenup Gill follow a clear path – part of the Coast-to-Coast walk – all the way back to Rosthwaite, which you join at a surfaced lane below Hazel Bank. Turn left and cross a bridge spanning Stonethwaite Beck, and walk out to the main road. Go left, and shortly right to return to the start. ●

Mallard and chicks

Troutbeck Valley

		GPS waypoints	
Start	Troutbeck		NY 412 027
Distance	6 miles (9.5km); including The Tongue 7¾ miles (12.5km)	Ⓐ	NY 417 027
Height gain	855 feet (260m); including The Tongue 1,330 feet (405m)	Ⓑ	NY 426 064
		Ⓒ	NY 421 054
Approximate time	3 hours; including The Tongue 4 hours	Ⓓ	NY 416 039
		Ⓔ	NY 412 033
Parking	Church bridge		
Route terrain	Rough fell tracks and lanes		
Ordnance Survey maps	Landranger 90 (Penrith & Keswick), Explorer OL7 (The English Lakes – South-eastern area)		

The valley of Troutbeck probes a slender finger northwards from Windermere shore towards the smooth-sided fells of Kentmere and Caudale Moor. This is an ancient through-route over the Kirkstone Pass and into Patterdale and as such few visitors stop to explore the dale. This walk invites such exploration, making a simple tour of the valley, and visiting the largest farm owned by Beatrix Potter. An extension offers the opportunity to 'bag' The Tongue, a small but significant summit at the head of the valley. Since 1980, Troutbeck has been a conservation area, and those who appreciate vernacular architecture will delight in what the valley has to offer.

From the parking area, turn right to cross the footbridge beside Church Bridge, and walk alongside the road for

Jesus Church, Troutbeck

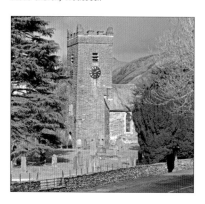

about 100 yds. Cross the road and head up the stony track opposite. Follow the track as it climbs steadily upwards, and continues easily, later merging with another coming in from the right. Just after this junction Ⓐ, the track forks. Bear left down to a gate, and take a now descending path that runs across the fell slopes above Limefitt Park, with The Tongue and the upper Troutbeck Valley now in view ahead.

Keep on past Long Green Head Farm, and stay with the ongoing track beyond, which is perfectly clear and presses on steadily, but gradually slims down to a footpath as it heads into the recesses of Hagg Gill between The Tongue and the smooth-sided Kentmere fells.

At a gate, just level with the southern end of The Tongue, it is possible to shortcut the walk a little by going through the gate, turning immediately left through another gate and then heading down to a footbridge across Hagg Gill, beyond which you ascend to the return track on the opposite side.

To extend the walk a little, simply keep on the original path, which takes you farther into Hagg Gill. Stay with the track as far as a footbridge spanning the gill, close by a stone barn. Cross the bridge and walk up to a gate **B** where you join the return track, now heading south to a gate where those who went up The Tongue will rejoin the route – see over.

(Strong walkers wanting to make more of the day can turn right on reaching the track, and follow it northwards for about 1 mile until, just before you encounter a wall, you can swing left to climb onto the northern end of The Tongue. There is a quad bike track and a path, but neither is especially necessary. Once on the ridge, a grassy path runs all the way south to the fine cairn on the summit of the fell. Beyond this a steep path goes down to a lower 'summit', and on down again until you cross a fence by a step-stile, after which the path gradually swings down to the left to rejoin the main path below. This is a lovely extension, and should be included in the walk if possible.)

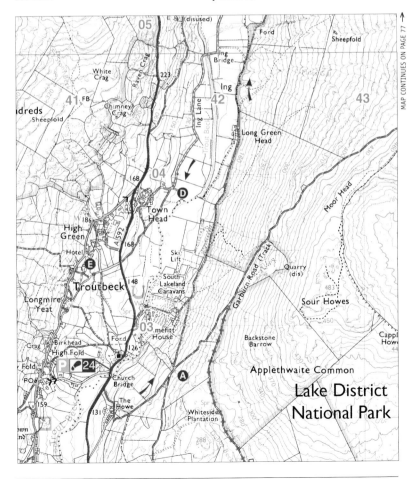

MAP CONTINUES ON PAGE 77

The Tongue

Continue with the main track, which shortly starts to descend, until you reach a wall corner. A few strides farther on, leave the main track by going through a kissing-gate on the left onto a path for Troutbeck village. This takes you down across a sloping grassy pasture, keeping to the left of Hall Hill, a large grassy mound.

This area is Troutbeck Park, linked to the nearby farm, one that has always been a large sheep farm. In 1923, the farm came up for sale, and was under threat of development. However, Beatrix Potter, who for the previous ten years had observed the functions of the dutiful wife of a country solicitor, living at Near Sawrey, decided to buy the farm. Three years after she bought it, she decided to run the farm herself with the aid of George Walker, shepherd brother-in-law of Tom Storey, who ran Hill Top Farm in Sawrey. Together, Walker and Potter built up a celebrated flock of Herdwick sheep, a small and hardy breed indigenous to the Lake District. When she died in 1943, Beatrix Potter left 14 farms and 4,000 acres of land to the National Trust.

The descending path reaches the farm access at Hagg Bridge **C**, and thereafter follows a surfaced route to Ing Bridge and onward towards Troutbeck village. Later, when the lane turns right to go up to Town Head, leave it by branching left onto a bridleway **D** between walls. The bridleway comes out to meet the valley road. Cross, and go into the lane opposite that leads up to Troutbeck.

When the lane swings to the right **E**, leave it by branching left onto a path for the church. When confronted by two gates, take that on the right, passing through a kissing-gate to follow the ongoing path beside a wall. Shortly the path narrows and runs down between fences. The path is straightforward and leads down to intercept a broad track. Turn left along the side of the graveyard and walk out to the road, there turning right to walk the short distance back to Church Bridge to complete the walk.

The origins of Troutbeck's church are lost, but it certainly existed in the 16th century. In the *Records relating to the Barony of Kendale,* it is recorded on 18 July 1562: 'Whereas Troutbeck is distant and remote from the parish church of St Martin's Windermere, the space of three myles soe that they cann neither bring the bodyes of the dead to be buryed att their parish church without their great and extraordinary cost and discommoditye nor carrye

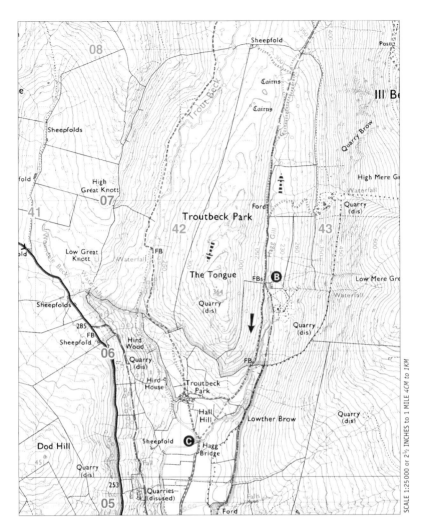

SCALE 1:25000 or 2½ INCHES to 1 MILE 4CM to 1KM

their children to be baptized without great danger of soul and bodye, nor can they by any means come to hear Divine Service, to receive the Sacrament nor to be instructed in the word of God as becometh Christians, without their so great cost, travel, danger and incommodity, William Downham, Bp. of Chester, licenced the newly rebuilt Chapel of Jesus at Troutbeck for the celebration of the Sacraments etc., with the consent "of that worshiful man Mr Adam Carehouse", rector of Windermere'.

The key aspects of this record are that in 1562, the chapel was 'newly rebuilt', clearly implying that a chapel existed at an earlier date.

The present church was dismantled and rebuilt in 1736, allegedly on the site of a 15th-century chapel. Major restoration was carried out by the Victorians in 1861, and much of the church now displays work of the Arts and Crafts Movement, notably that of Edward Burne-Jones and William Morris. Unusually, the church is not dedicated to a saint, but is known simply as Jesus Church.

TROUTBECK VALLEY • 77

Haweswater shore path

Haweswater shore path

		GPS waypoints	
Start	Burnbanks		NY 508 161
Distance	10 miles (16.3km)	Ⓐ	NY 487 154
Height gain	1,273 feet (388m)	Ⓑ	NY 468 118
Approximate time	4½ hours	Ⓒ	NY 479 118
Parking	Limited parking opposite telephone box. Please do not obstruct garages	Ⓓ	NY 479 130
		Ⓔ	NY 499 153
		Ⓕ	NY 510 160
Route terrain	Entirely low level, on good tracks and paths throughout most of the route		
Ordnance Survey maps	Landranger 90 (Penrith & Keswick), Explorer OL5 (The English Lakes – North-eastern area)		

Although long stretches of this circular walk had been in use for some time – the north shore route is part of the Northern Coast-to-Coast Walk – only during 1995, was a complete link made possible in a partnership between the National Park Authority and what was then North West Water. Haweswater is the highest lake in the Lake District at 790 ft (240m), and the fourth deepest. The route concludes through Naddle Forest, a nature reserve and Site of Special Scientific Interest, where the red squirrel still survives; and passes other land managed by the Royal Society for the Protection of Birds, home to many rare species, including the golden eagle.

Set off from Burnbanks by walking up a rough lane to the right of the telephone box, to pass cottages. The cottages were built to accommodate men working on the reservoir and dam, and although once falling into disrepair in recent times they have been restored. After the last of the cottages, go forward to a gate at which you enter light woodland. Follow a broad trail right and then left to a gate in a boundary fence.

Beyond the gate the track continues along the woodland boundary and across the base of open, craggy slopes clad in bracken, and dotted with hawthorn, rowan and gorse. The track climbs gently to a level section, where the reservoir, glimpsed through trees, comes into view along with, ahead on the right, the hanging valley of Fordingdale, through which flows Measand Beck.

The track continues uneventfully, but no less a joy to walk, accompanied either by a wall or a fence, and rising on the right to a conspicuous cairn on Four Stones Hill. A stretch of clear ground on the left allows a fine view up the length of Haweswater to the ring of summits at its head.

Near the ruins of a homestead, the broad track ends and becomes a narrow path, descending to cross streams before reaching the rocky gorge containing

Haweswater

Measand Beck . A bridge takes you over the beck, followed by a short rise to cross the low end of Sandhill Knotts before running on across more open fellside rising steeply on the right to the vast moorland reaches of High Raise and Long Grain.

Pleasant walking ensues on the approach to the great hollow of Whelter Bottom traversing steep slopes, undulating in delightful fashion. Finally, the path descends through bracken, beside which more collapsed stone walls leading down to the water's edge from the intake wall remind again that an isolated farming community once lived and worked in Mardale. A sturdy footbridge crosses Whelter Beck, cascading down a narrow ravine lined with holly bushes, rowan and alder. Above, the broken form of Whelter Crag rises steeply on the right, its grassy flanks often grazed by red deer.

Beyond the footbridge, the path heads for the intake wall before moving away to cross the snout of Birks Crag and Castle Crag, the site of an ancient British hill fort. The ongoing path now descends steeply as it approaches Riggindale, where it meanders through field enclosures, passing below a small wall-enclosed woodland. Rough Crag rises directly ahead and, as you round the edge of the woodland, the lower, craggy slopes of Kidsty Pike come into view. A sharp change of direction leads down to cross Randale Beck by a stone bridge, followed by a brief interlude of grassy terrain before a wooden footbridge across Riggindale Beck .

The path is then channelled between rows of low upright stones to reach a compact flight of steps and more upright stones leading to and through a small stand of larch. The way ahead now lies to the right of the prominent, wooded end of Rough Crag, known as The Rigg. Across this ridge, the path descends gently to find its way around the head of the lake, by footbridges and gates, to reach the car park at the roadhead.

At the northern edge of the car park go through a small gap in a low wall on to the signposted "Lakeshore Footpath: Burnbanks". Not far along this early leg

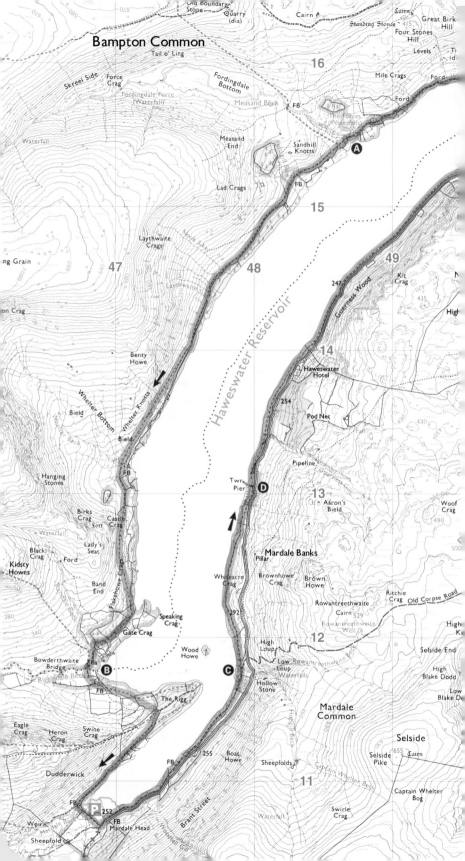

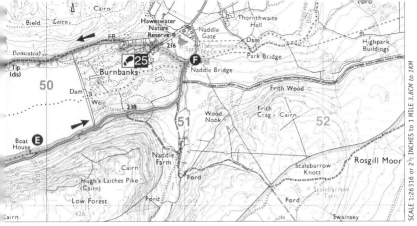

SCALE 1:26316 or 2½ INCHES to 1 MILE 3.8CM to 1KM

0	200	400	600	800 METRES	**1**
					KILOMETRES
					MILES
0	200	400	600 YARDS	½	

of the return journey, the path passes above the spot where the Dun Bull Hotel once stood, lost forever in a physical sense, but still of fond memory as a meeting place for shepherds and the people of these remote fells. In conditions of extreme drought, such as prevailed in 1984, the walls of the village lie exposed once more.

Throughout its entire length the path never strays far from the road wall, often pressing close up beside it, a visually limiting factor of no importance since all the views, and stunning they are, lie across the reservoir, into Riggindale, Whelter Bottom and, later, Fordingdale. For much of its course, the path undulates, dipping and diving through old enclosures to reach a footbridge spanning Hopgill Beck **C**.

Cross the bridge, and at a wall gap, follow the path ahead (signposted to Burnbanks). The path climbs out of the gill and then contours across slopes of bracken, hawthorn and holly. As the path approaches a reservoir control tower it enters woodland. There used to be a diversion here to take the path up to the wall, away from the vicinity of the tower, but this is less evident now, and walkers appear to be permitted to walk past the tower **D**, even though the concessionary path is still shown at a higher level on maps, as is the boundary of Access Land. The tower is the draw-

off point for the reservoir, and a building largely constructed from the remains of Mardale village church. A short way farther on, as the service track rises to the road, leave it by branching left back along the shore path.

Now you engage some delightful prime woodland, mainly birch, sycamore and beech, and encounter a number of places where the path crosses narrow ledges above steep drops to the reservoir. Frequently, as if afraid to leave its protection, the path clings to the wall, and, as a result, you pass by the **Haweswater Hotel** almost unaware of its existence. Elsewhere, the path meanders through the lowest edges of Guerness Wood, where raised tree roots can trip the unwary, or the weary.

With the dam in sight, the path weaves behind an old boathouse, before finally rising to the road at a gate **E**.

On the road, go left, and follow it round as far as Naddle Bridge **F**. Cross the bridge, and immediately turn left over a stone stile into oak woodland, a sylvan glade that for west-east Coast-to-Coast walkers effectively marks the end of Lakeland and the start of the limestone fringe en route for Kirkby Stephen. Within the woodland the path forks; either way will take you back to the edge of Burnbanks.

The Langdale valleys

Start	Great Langdale, New Dungeon Ghyll	**GPS waypoints**	
Distance	8½ miles (13.5km)	�	NY 294 064
Height gain	1,690 feet (515m)	Ⓐ	NY 289 051
		Ⓑ	NY 300 032
Approximate time	4½ hours	Ⓒ	NY 312 029
Parking	Stickle Ghyll car park (National Trust Pay and Display)	Ⓓ	NY 321 041
		Ⓔ	NY 308 057
Route terrain	Rough fell paths; woodland; some road walking		
Ordnance Survey maps	Landranger 90 (Penrith & Keswick), Explorers OL6 (The English Lakes – South-western area) and OL7 (The English Lakes – South-eastern area)		

The two Langdale valleys – Great and Little – are separated by the craggy bulk of Lingmoor Fell, and combining them offers a succession of fine views. The Langdale Pikes dominate much of the first part of the walk, along with the headwall of Great Langdale in the form of Crinkle Crags and Bowfell. But once you pass into Little Langdale it is the Coniston Fells, notably Wetherlam and Swirl How that ease into view; that they are seen from an unusual angle makes them all the more interesting.

🔳 The walk begins from the Stickle Ghyll car park in Great Langdale by walking up to the left of the buildings at the rear of the car park to access a brief, enclosed path that soon leads out to a junction of paths at Stickle Ghyll. Where the track divides, bear left and rise steadily to a gate. Beyond, the path divides again. Keep left again, now descending to cross a footbridge.

Almost immediately you encounter a feature known as the Ring Garth, a circle of great walls around the valley enclosing the arable land in the valley bottom. The garth, which can still be traced around most of the valley, takes the form of the stone wall on your right, which is composed of a higher incidence of large and in situ boulders than the comparatively juvenile wall on

your left. This distinction becomes more evident the farther along the valley you travel, and it hallmarks the time of Norse settlement after the 10th century. Certainly the ring garth was in place by the early 13th century, when a document refers to the 'inclosed land of Great Langden' under which it was granted to Conishead Priory.

The first evidence of human activity in Langdale, however, is associated with Neolithic axe factories on the high slopes of the Langdale Pikes, which are thought to have been in use from around 6,000 years ago. What makes these axe factories particularly noteworthy is that they mark a change of lifestyle among our prehistoric ancestors from hunter-gatherers, always on the move, to a more settled period when static farming in the valleys freed the axe makers from the necessities of the hunt.

When you reach Old Dungeon Ghyll, the first of the properties in Langdale acquired by the National Trust, in 1929, go through a gate and follow the track down to the car park. Bear right along the car park access to meet a surfaced lane. Go left over a road bridge spanning Great Langdale Beck to a T-junction. Turn right to another junction, and there turn left, walking along the road, but only as far as the entrance to a campsite on the left, next to a fine specimen of a pollarded ash tree.

Go into the campsite, on a footpath for Side Pike and Lingmoor Fell. Follow the right-hand wall to cross a footbridge, and then leave the site as the path begins to climb the fellside above. After a narrow pasture you enter a small larch plantation. Climb through the plantation, leaving it at a gate to press on steeply beside a wall. Eventually the track levels as it moves on to a ladder-stile over which you join the road **A**, linking the two Langdale valleys, and with Blea Tarn now suddenly coming into view.

Cross the road and walk with a wall on your left to a gate through which the lovely path to Blea Tarn begins. Follow the path beyond Blea Tarn, and when it divides, ignore the footbridge on the left, and bear right to gate/wall giving out onto the great expanse of Blea Moss. Now descend alongside Bleamoss Beck, the path later running parallel with a wall. But when the wall changes direction, bear off to the right, continuing with the main path that runs out to meet the Wrynose Pass road. As you approach the road, the path sinks

Little Langdale Beck at Slater Bridge

into marshy ground, but without any detriment to route finding.

On reaching the road, turn left and follow it down to Fell Foot Farm. On the way you pass two notable features: one, the evident volcanic upthrust of Castle Howe, site of a Neolithic hill fort, the other (accessed by a gate just above Fell Foot) known as a Ting Mound.

The Ting Mound, sometimes Thing Mound, or Thing Moot, is an open-air court, meeting place, or parliament, used by those responsible for the administration of the countryside. Generally, they appear to date from the 7th-9th centuries, and some are recorded in the *Domesday Book,* suggesting a continuing use into the medieval period.

Fell Foot Farm is also interesting. Dating from the 17th century, this was originally a coaching inn, reputedly used as a hideaway for illicit goods

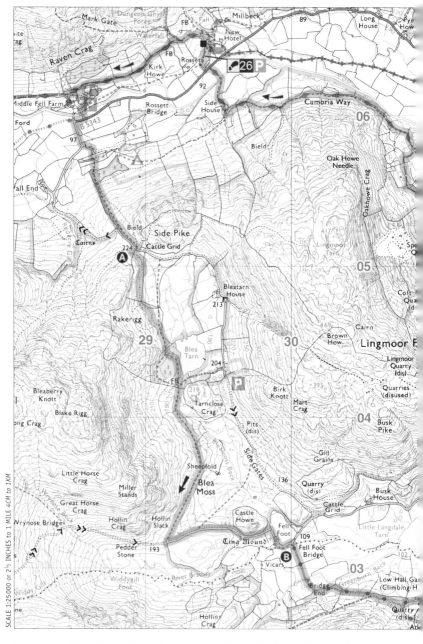

SCALE 1:25 000 or 2½ INCHES to 1 MILE 4CM to 1KM

0	200	400	600	800 METRES	1
					KILOMETRES
					MILES
0	200	400	600 YARDS	½	

smuggled over the fells. Beatrix Potter was responsible for reviving the fortunes of Fell Foot as a place of accommodation and hospitality when, while working as a land agent for the National Trust, she did much to persuade hill farmers to start taking in visitors to augment their income.

Stay along the road after leaving Fell Foot Farm until you reach Fell Foot Bridge **B** on the right, which spans the infant River Brathay. Cross this and now take to a broad track across flat pastures

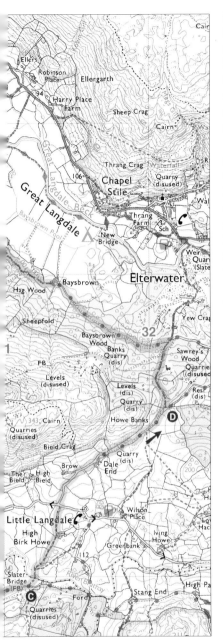

stone-built structure. Low Hall Garth lies a short way farther on beyond an area of slate spoil, a reminder that this is mining country. After the cottages, the track levels as it leads on to a gate on the left **C** giving onto Slater Bridge, a typical packhorse bridge spanning the Brathay.

Beyond the bridge, follow an ascending path beside a wall that eventually leads up to High Birk Howe Farm. Turn left and follow the farm access out to a lane. Turn left and immediately right into a side lane leading up to Dale Head, after which the road surfacing ends and the ongoing track becomes stony and uneven.

Just after a gate the track forks **D**, with the main track continuing its descent to Elterwater. Bear left at this point, ascending easily into woodland and passing what might be called a 'Money Tree' – it's self-evident when you find it.

Following a short ascent the path descends between luxurious moss-covered walls. Keep following the track until you reach a cottage and a narrow surfaced lane. Turn left here, and now follow the lane through delightful light woodland to reach Baysbrown Farm. There continue along the bridleway for Oak Howe.

Shortly, when the track forks, keep left, and at the next divide, go right. Another splendid path takes you on through the woodland, and then down to the group of buildings at Oak Howe **E**. At a signpost turn left for New Dungeon Ghyll. The ongoing path is straightforward and provides fine views of the Langdale Pikes and the head of Langdale. Continue with the path on a clear and obvious route to Side House Farm.

Now all that remains is to follow the farm access out to the main valley road, which you join close by the starting point. ⬤

to reach another neat bridge beside a cottage, spanning Greenburn Beck.

Beyond the cottage the track rises gently across a fell shoulder. High above Little Langdale Tarn, the track forks. Here branch left heading down to a walled track that passes High Hallgarth cottage, a 17th-century

Black Combe

Start	Whicham	GPS waypoints
Distance	8½ miles (13.5km). Shorter version 5 miles (8km)	SD 135 826
		Ⓐ SD 131 828
Height gain	2,185 feet (666m). Shorter version 1,853 feet (565m)	Ⓑ SD 134 853
		Ⓒ SD 117 870
Approximate time	4½ hours. Shorter version 3 hours	Ⓓ SD 125 828
Parking	Lay-by on the A595, near Whicham church, or, on days when there is no church service, there is a larger parking area adjacent to the church	
Route terrain	Rugged fell tops and tracks; *not advised in poor visibility*	
Ordnance Survey maps	Landranger 96 (Barrow-in-Furness & South Lakeland), Explorer OL6 (The English Lakes – South-western area)	

The beauty of Black Combe is not its face, which is rather plain, but its unrivalled views, unimpeded by intervening hills or woodlands. This is a scintillating, connoisseur's fell, achieved by a clean and simple line that is never in doubt. The fell does not quite achieve the notoriety that a height of 2,000 ft brings, but it just tops 600m, which, for want of a better excuse, is reason enough to visit this isolated top.
Many walkers want simply to return from the summit – although there are actually two summits, one with a massive cairn – and that is a fine enough excursion. But this walk offers a much longer expedition that wanders off into the voluptuous embrace of the north-western fell slopes.

Walk to the church, and go past it into a narrow pathway that emerges onto a very narrow lane leading up to Kirkbank. Turn left at the lane, and walk up to the farm. Keep to the right of the buildings and walk into an enclosed track that runs around the farm boundary to reach open fell Ⓐ. Here the track forks. Turn right and walk up to a gate/stile. After that, the way is never in doubt and climbs incessantly upwards. There is a brief steeper section quite early on, but after that the ascent is gradual. However, the wide path you

are following does not take you to the summit. To reach that, you must leave the path at a bend Ⓑ, and walk up an easy slope to the trig pillar surrounded by a stone shelter and with the most breathtaking view into the heart of the Lakeland fells.

To the south, beyond an intervening tarn, there lies a slightly lower summit, but one that has a massive cairn. From this hoary fell top in distant wardening

0	200	400	600	800 METRES	1	
						KILOMETRES
						MILES
0	200	400	600 YARDS	½		

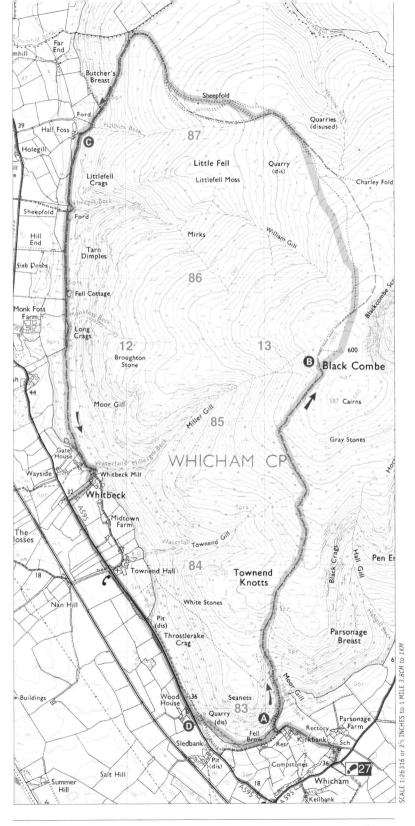

Far End

Broomhill Beck

Butcher's
Breast

Sheepfold

Quarries
(dis used)

Ford

Hallfoss Beck

87

Quarry
(dis)

Charley Fold

Hall Foss
39

C

Little Fell
Littlefell Moss

Holegill

Littlefell
Crags

Sheepfold

Holegill Beck

Ford

Mirks

William Gill

Hill
End

Tarn
Dimples

86

Fish Ponds

Fell Cottage

Monk Foss
Farm

Long
Crags

Monkfoss Beck

12

Broughton
Stone

13

B Black Combe

600

44

Moor Gill

587 Cairns

Miller Gill

Gray Stones

85

Gate
House

Miller Gill Beck

WHICHAM CP

Wayside

Waterfalls

Whitbeck Mill

32

Whitbeck

Midtown
Farm

Waterfall

Townend Gill

Black Crags

Hall Gill

Pen E

The
losses

Townend Hall

84

Townend
Knotts

18

Nan Hill

White Stones

Parsonage
Breast

Pit
(dis)

Throstlerake
Crag

Buildings

Wood
House

36

Seaness

83

Moor Gill

A

Quarry
(dis)

D

Fell
Brow

Resr

Rectory

Parsonage
Farm

Sch

Sledbank

Kirkbank

Pit
(dis)

Cumpstones

36

27

Salt Hill

Summer
Hill

Whicham

4

A595

Kellbank

SCALE 1:26316 or 2½ INCHES to 1 MILE 3.8CM to 1KM

Whicham church

days, the author accomplished the 'Most Unusual Mountain Rescue of the Year' by carrying back to Whicham tucked inside his anorak what at first glance had been just another iced rock in the enormous cairn. In reality it was a sad and sorrowful cat that had somehow found its way onto the fell top, and would surely have died had he not chanced along and shared his coffee with it. On reaching Kirkbank, the cat skittered away into the farm buildings.

From the top of Black Combe you can simply retreat the way you came, and many do. *But to tackle the longer walk, leave the summit by heading northwards.* An indistinct path starts from the trig, but then improves, becoming a quad bike track. Take care not to descend too far to the right (east), as there is a similar path heading down Black Combe ridge. Once on the correct track – it runs roughly north-westwards, but not quite as the line marked on the map until much lower down – it is simply a question of following its easy and untroubled course until it finally descends almost to a wall, where it intercepts another track overlooking Bootle, with Barfield Tarn clearly in view to the left.

Turn left and walk beside a fence. An earlier shortcut from the higher track brings you down to the fence also.

Continue alongside the fence, and then a wall and descend towards the ruins of Hall Foss Farm **C**. Here turn left to discover that the path is now a delightful green track beside the wall, one that leads on to cross deeply incised Holegill Beck, which may require a bit of nifty boulder hopping to cross dry-shod.

Resume the wallside track, which leads up past derelict Fell Cottage before pressing on to cross the base of Monkfoss Beck, which displays a couple of neat waterfalls. When the track, which is now a green swathe through bracken, forks (SD 115 854), keep left, sticking to the higher ground.

Eventually the track comes down to run beside a wall above the farms at Whitbeck. Here, keep alongside the wall and pass above the farms to reach Whitbeck Mill below the waterfalls of Millergill Beck. Follow a rough lane past cottages and farms, which after a cattle-grid becomes a pronounced vehicle track. The lane runs out to meet the A595. Turn left and walk beside the road, using verges as much as possible, and always taking care against approaching traffic. This short bout of unpleasantness is the price you pay for the pleasure of what has gone before. The roadside public footpath shown on maps does not exist on the ground; *so great care is needed here as you follow the road for almost one mile.*

At **D**, leave the road by climbing a steep bank on the left, and soon bearing right to cross a fell shoulder. The path eventually descends to run alongside a wall, and shortly a vehicle access. Keep forward along this, and soon you will meet the outward route. Walk down the lane and take the narrow path past the church to complete the walk. ●

Bowfell

Start	Great Langdale	GPS waypoints
Distance	7½ miles (12km)	✏ NY 286 061
Height gain	2,855 feet (870m)	Ⓐ NY 276 057
Approximate time	4½ hours	Ⓑ NY 248 060
Parking	Old Dungeon Ghyll	Ⓒ NY 240 072
Route terrain	Rough mountain fell tracks; *not advised in poor visibility*	Ⓓ NY 247 075
		Ⓔ NY 261 074
Ordnance Survey maps	Landranger 90 (Penrith & Keswick), Explorer OL6 (The English Lakes – South-western area)	

All the high fells of Langdale are popular; Bowfell, being the highest, is in consequence an experience you will have to share with someone else. But it is a huge fell, and there is plenty of room in which to lose yourself, which is an excellent reason for not attempting Bowfell in anything other than clear conditions. *With Bowfell it is not height that is the draw, but rather the long approach via The Band, the ascent of rocky slopes, the exploration of the trek across towards Esk Pike, the final, long walk out down Rossett Gill and through delectable Mickleden, and, of course, the stunning views.*

✏ Walk out from the Old Dungeon Ghyll car park to cross a bridge and reach the valley road. Turn right to a point where the road changes direction, and here leave the road and walk ahead onto the broad farm access leading to Stool End.

Pass between the farm buildings to gain the open fellside. Ignore the track branching off to the right into Mickleden, and turn briefly towards Oxendale, then look for a clear and substantially renovated path Ⓐ setting off up The Band. The path rises to a wall and kissing-gate from where there is a fine view of Pike of Stickle and its immense scree run.

The route up The Band generally keeps to the Oxendale side, but occasionally wanders over to take a peek into Mickleden. Towards the top, and just after Bowfell comes into view, you reach a grassy plateau. Beyond that, the trail continues an uneventful rise to the col between Bowfell and Crinkle Crags, wherein lie the Three Tarns Ⓑ. The crags of Bowfell Links are especially prominent now, as, too, are the highest summits of England, Scafell Pike and Scafell, seen off to the west across the vast boggy bowl known as Great Moss.

From the col a rough stony ascent brings you to the top of Bowfell. Bowfell was described in 1902, by F.G. Brabant in *The English Lakes* as '... conspicuous among the lake mountains for its graceful, tapering peak ... It is a wild and rocky, though not very precipitous mountain, and the confused

Wall End Farm, Langdale Pikes and Mickleden

way in which its top is strewn with rock-masses is only equalled by Scafell Pikes. Few of the lake mountains are

better worth ascending'.

The speediest and surest return to Langdale is back the way you came, but to continue the walk, leave the summit in a northerly direction taking a cairned

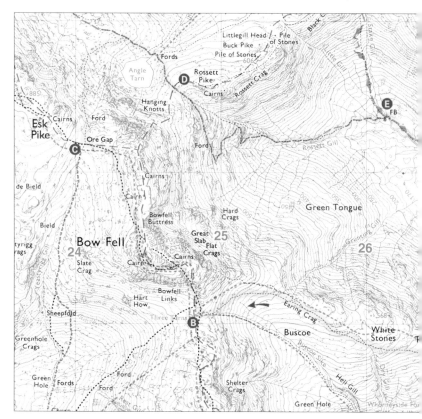

crags of Esk Pike, aiming to the west of Angle Tarn, around which a path circles to intercept a much more substantial track below Tongue Head, an ancient route across the fells and more than likely the way stone axes manufactured on Langdale's slopes were taken out to the coast.

From Angle Tarn, beautifully set against the crags of Hanging Knotts, the path rises a little as it heads for a gap **D** to the south of Rossett Pike. Beyond, a much-restored path zigzags into the head of Mickleden, slipping downwards to meet the Cumbria Way at a wooden footbridge **E** at the foot of the Stake Pass. Now all that remains is to follow a straightforward route in a south-easterly direction back to Old Dungeon Ghyll. ●

and steadily descending route to another col, Ore Gap **C**. *Pay close attention to the route to Ore Gap as it is easy to wander off line.*

From the col descend beneath the

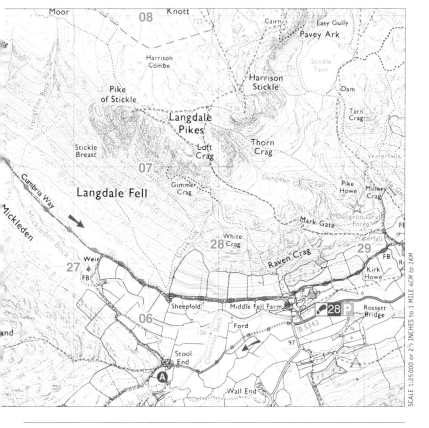

Further Information

Safety on the Hills

The hills, mountains and moorlands of Britain, though of modest height compared with those in many other countries, need to be treated with respect. Friendly and inviting in good weather, they can quickly be transformed into wet, misty, windswept and potentially dangerous areas of wilderness in bad weather. Even on an outwardly fine and settled summer day, conditions can rapidly deteriorate at high altitudes and, in winter, even more so.

Therefore it is advisable to always take both warm and waterproof clothing, sufficient nourishing food, a hot drink, first-aid kit, torch and whistle. Wear suitable footwear, such as strong walking-boots or shoes that give a good grip over rocky terrain and on slippery slopes. Try to obtain a local weather forecast and bear it in mind before you start. Do not be afraid to abandon your proposed route and return to your starting point in the event of a sudden and unexpected deterioration in the weather. Do not go alone and allow enough time to finish the walk well before nightfall.

Most of the walks described in this book do not venture into remote wilderness areas and will be safe to do, given due care and respect, at any time of year in all but the most unreasonable weather. Indeed, a crisp, fine winter day often provides perfect walking conditions, with firm ground underfoot and a clarity that is not possible to achieve in the other seasons of the year. A few walks, however, are suitable only for reasonably fit and experienced hill walkers able to use a compass and should definitely not be tackled by anyone else during the winter months or in bad weather, especially high winds and mist. These are indicated in the general description that precedes each of the walks.

Walkers and the Law

The Countryside and Rights of Way Act (CRoW Act 2000) extends the rights of access previously enjoyed by walkers in England and Wales. Implementation of these rights began on 19 September 2004. The Act amends existing legislation and for the first time provides access on foot to certain types of land – defined as mountain, moor, heath, down and registered common land.

Where You Can Go
Rights of Way
Prior to the introduction of the CRoW Act, walkers could only legally access the countryside along public rights of way. These are either 'footpaths' (for walkers only) or 'bridleways' (for walkers, riders on horseback and pedal cyclists). A third category called 'Byways open to all traffic' (BOATs), is used by motorised vehicles as well as those using non-mechanised transport. Mainly they are green lanes, farm and estate roads, although occasionally they will be found crossing mountainous area.

Rights of way are marked on Ordnance Survey maps. Look for the green broken lines on the Explorer maps, or the red dashed lines on Landranger maps.

The term 'right of way' means exactly what it says. It gives a right of passage over what, for the most part, is private land. Under pre-CRoW legislation walkers were required to keep to the line of the right of way and not stray onto land on either side. If you did inadvertently wander off the right of way, either because of faulty map reading or because the route was not clearly indicated on the ground, you were technically trespassing.

Local authorities have a legal obligation to ensure that rights of way are kept clear and free of obstruction, and are signposted where they leave metalled roads. The duty of local authorities to install signposts extends to the placing of signs along a path or way, but only where the authority considers it necessary to have a signpost or waymark to assist persons unfamiliar with the locality.

Countryside Access Charter

Your rights of way are:

- public footpaths – on foot only. Sometimes waymarked in yellow
- bridleways – on foot, horseback and pedal cycle. Sometimes waymarked in blue
- byways (usually old roads), most 'roads used as public paths' and, of course, public roads – all traffic has the right of way

Use maps, signs and waymarks to check rights of way. Ordnance Survey Explorer and Landranger maps show most public rights of way

On rights of way you can:

- take a pram, pushchair or wheelchair if practicable
- take a dog (on a lead or under close control)
- take a short route round an illegal obstruction or remove it sufficiently to get past

You have a right to go for recreation to:

- public parks and open spaces – on foot
- most commons near older towns and cities – on foot and sometimes on horseback
- private land where the owner has a formal agreement with the local authority

In addition you can use the following by local or established custom or consent, but ask for advice if you are unsure:

- many areas of open country, such as moorland, fell and coastal areas, especially those in the care of the National Trust, and some commons
- some woods and forests, especially those owned by the Forestry Commission
- country parks and picnic sites
- most beaches
- canal towpaths
- some private paths and tracks Consent sometimes extends to horse-riding and cycling

For your information:

- county councils and London boroughs maintain and record rights of way, and register commons
- obstructions, dangerous animals, harassment and misleading signs on rights of way are illegal and you should report them to the county council
- paths across fields can be ploughed, but must normally be reinstated within two weeks
- landowners can require you to leave land to which you have no right of access
- motor vehicles are normally permitted only on roads, byways and some 'roads used as public paths'

Further Information

The New Access Rights
Access Land

As well as being able to walk on existing rights of way, under the new legislation you now have access to large areas of open land. You can of course continue to use rights of way footpaths to cross this land, but the main difference is that you can now lawfully leave the path and wander at will, but only in areas designated as access land.

Where to Walk

Areas now covered by the new access rights – Access Land – are shown on Ordnance Survey Explorer maps by a light yellow tint surrounded by a pale orange border. New orange coloured 'i' symbols

on the maps will show the location of permanent access information boards installed by the access authorities.

Restrictions

The right to walk on access land may lawfully be restricted by landowners. Landowners can, for any reason, restrict access for up to 28 days in any year. They cannot however close the land:

- on bank holidays;
- for more than four Saturdays and Sundays in a year;
- on any Saturday from 1 June to 11 August; or
- on any Sunday from 1 June to the end of September.

  They have to provide local authorities

Further Information

with five working days' notice before the date of closure unless the land involved is an area of less than five hectares or the closure is for less than four hours. In these cases land-owners only need to provide two hours' notice.

Whatever restrictions are put into place on access land they have no effect on existing rights of way, and you can continue to walk on them.

Dogs

Dogs can be taken on access land, but must be kept on leads of two metres or less between 1 March and 31 July, and at all times where they are near livestock. In addition landowners may impose a ban on all dogs from fields where lambing takes place for up to six weeks in any year. Dogs may be banned from moorland used for grouse shooting and breeding for up to five years.

In the main, walkers following the routes in this book will continue to follow existing rights of way, but a knowledge and understanding of the law as it affects walkers, plus the ability to distinguish access land marked on the maps, will enable anyone who wishes to depart from paths that cross access land either to take a shortcut, to enjoy a view or to explore.

General Obstructions

Obstructions can sometimes cause a problem on a walk and the most common of these is where the path across a field has been ploughed over. It is legal for a farmer to plough up a path provided that it is restored within two weeks. This does not always happen and you are faced with the dilemma of following the line of the path, even if this means treading on crops, or walking round the edge of the field. Although the later course of action seems the most sensible, it does mean that you would be trespassing.

Other obstructions can vary from overhanging vegetation to wire fences across the path, locked gates or even a cattle feeder on the path.

Use common sense. If you can get round the obstruction without causing

damage, do so. Otherwise only remove as much of the obstruction as is necessary to secure passage.

If the right of way is blocked and cannot be followed, there is a long-standing view that in such circumstances there is a right to deviate, but this cannot wholly be relied on. Although it is accepted in law that highways (and that includes rights of way) are for the public service, and if the usual track is impassable, it is for the general good that people should be entitled to pass into another line. However, this should not be taken as indicating a right to deviate whenever a way becomes impassable. If in doubt, retreat.

Report obstructions to the local authority and/or the Ramblers.

 Useful Organisations

Campaign for National Parks
5-11 Lavington Street,
London, SE1 0NZ
Tel. 020 7981 0890
www.cnp.org.uk

Campaign to Protect Rural England (CPRE)
5-11 Lavington Street,
London SE1 0NZ
Tel. 020 7981 2800
www.cpre.org.uk

Forestry Commission England
North West and West Midlands Area office
Tel. 0300 067 4190
www.forestry.gov.uk

Friends of the Lake District
Murley Moss, Oxenholme Road,
Kendal, Cumbria
LA9 7SS
Tel. 01539 720788
www.friendsofthelakedistrict.org.uk

Tourist Information Centres
(*not open all year)*:
Ambleside: 015394 32582
Bowness Bay: 015394 42895
*Broughton-in-Furness: 01229 716115
Cockermouth: 01900 822634

Coniston: 015394 41533
Egremont: 01946 820693
*Glenridding: 017684 82414
Grasmere: 015394 35245
Hawkshead: 015394 36946
Kendal: 01539 735891
Keswick: 017687 72645
*Millom: 01229 772555
Penrith: 01768 867466
Waterhead: 015394 32729

**Lake District National Park
Visitor Centre**
Brockhole, Windermere,
Cumbria LA23 1LJ
Tel. 015394 46601
www.lakedistrict.gov.uk

Muncaster Castle
Usually closed Saturdays, check website
for details. Reduced rate tickets for
walkers who want to explore the grounds
are usually available at any ticket office.
Tel. 01229 717 614 in advance
www.muncaster.co.uk

National Trust
Membership and general enquiries:
Tel. 0344 800 1895
Lake District Regional Office:
The Hollens, Grasmere,
Ambleside, Cumbria LA22 9QZ
Tel. 015394 35599
www.nationaltrust.org.uk

Natural England
Kendal Office, Juniper House,
Murley Moss, Oxenholme Road,
Kendal, LA9 7RL
Tel. 0300 060 3900
www.gov.uk/government/organisations/
natural-england

Ordnance Survey
Tel. 03456 05 05 05 (Lo-call)
www.ordnancesurvey.co.uk

Ramblers
2nd Floor, Camelford House, 87–90
Albert Embankment, London SE1 7TW
Tel. 020 7339 8500
www.ramblers.org.uk

Visit Cumbria
www.visitcumbria.com

Youth Hostels Association
Trevelyan House, Dimple Road,
Matlock, Derbyshire
DE4 3YH
Tel. 01629 592700
www.yha.org.uk

 *Ordnance Survey maps of the
Lake District*
The Lake District is covered by Ordnance
Survey 1:50 000 (1$\frac{1}{4}$ inches to 1 mile or
2cm to 1km) scale Landranger map sheets
85, 86, 89, 90, 91, 96, 97 and 98. These
all-purpose maps are packed with
information to help you explore the area.
Viewpoints, picnic sites, places of interest
and caravan and camping sites are shown,
as well as public rights of way information
such as footpaths and bridleways.

To examine the Lake District in more
detail, and especially if you are planning
walks, Ordnance Survey Explorer maps at
1:25 000 (2$\frac{1}{2}$ inches to 1 mile or 4cm to
1km) scale are ideal. Four such maps cover
the main Lake District National Park:

OL4 The English Lakes –
        North-western area
OL5 The English Lakes –
        North-eastern area
OL6 The English Lakes –
        South-western area

OL7 The English Lakes –
        South-eastern area

Ordnance Survey